CASEY WATSON

THE *SUNDAY TIMES* BESTSELLING AUTHOR

Groomed

**Danger lies closer
than you think**

This book is a work of non-fiction based on the author's experiences.
In order to protect privacy, names, identifying characteristics,
dialogue and details have been changed or reconstructed.

HarperElement
An imprint of HarperCollins*Publishers*
1 London Bridge Street
London SE1 9GF

www.harpercollins.co.uk

First published by HarperElement 2017

1 3 5 7 9 10 8 6 4 2

A catalogue record of this book is
available from the British Library

PB ISBN 978-0-00-821760-0
EB ISBN 978-0-00-821761-7

Printed and bound in Great Britain by
CPI Group (UK) Ltd, Croydon, CR0 4YY

MIX
Paper from
responsible sources

FSC
www.fsc.org

FSC™ C007454

FSC™ is a non-profit international organisation established to promote
the responsible management of the world's forests. Products carrying the
FSC label are independently certified to assure consumers that they come
from forests that are managed to meet the social, economic and
ecological needs of present and future generations,
and other controlled sources.

Find out more about HarperCollins and the environment at
www.harpercollins.co.uk/green

This book is dedicated to the army of passionate foster carers out there, each doing their bit to ensure that our children are kept as safe as possible in such a changing and often scary world. As technology is reinvented and becomes ever more complicated for those of us who were not brought up amid such advances, we can only try to keep up, in the hope that we continue to learn alongside our young people.

Acknowledgements

I remain endlessly grateful to my team at HarperCollins for their continuing support, and I'm especially excited to see the return of my editor, the very lovely Vicky Eribo, and look forward to sharing my new stories with her. As always, nothing would be possible without my wonderful agent, Andrew Lownie, the very best agent in the world in my opinion, and my grateful thanks also to the lovely Lynne, my friend and mentor forever.

Chapter 1

Mid-September. To me, always a melancholy time of year. Summer clinging on in bursts, the sun still trying to keep the air warm – but undermined by the chill creep of autumn once it sets, increasingly bullying its way into its rightful place.

I try to like autumn, what with the spectacular colours and all those lovely piles of crispy leaves. But it's not my favourite. In fact it's my least favourite season; sandwiched as it is between summer and Christmas, which isn't a season but, to my mind, ought to be. It always seems to take much too long to arrive and, once it does arrive, is always over much too quickly.

Still, autumn has a plus point, and that's the telly. And amid a slew of programmes that had returned from their summer break was the Saturday night ritual of *The Jonathan Ross Show*, a family favourite since way back when. Which was why, when my mobile buzzed, given the day and the timing, I thought it must be Riley who was calling.

Mike laughed. 'She knows you *so* well,' he said, chuckling, as I got off the sofa to go and fetch it. 'Heaven forbid you miss lover-boy.'

He was referring to the actor James McAvoy, who was one of the guests that night, and of course he was absolutely right.

'Cheek,' I called back to him as I disappeared into the kitchen. 'I just happen to think he's a particularly fine actor.'

'Course you do,' he answered as I reappeared in the doorway. 'Just like I admire Fiona Bruce for her brilliant journalism.'

But by this time I already knew that it wasn't Riley calling. The display on the phone said no number ID. Perhaps it was James McAvoy declaring his undying devotion.

It wasn't.

'Hello, is that Mrs Watson?' asked a female voice. 'Casey Watson?' I told her yes. 'Ah, good,' she said. 'Helena Curry here. EDT. Very glad to have managed to get hold of you. Am I right in thinking you might be available and free at the moment?'

I gestured with my hand that Mike should pause the TV. 'Yes,' I told her. 'We don't have anyone else in at the moment. Well, apart from our long-term foster son, of course.'

'Tyler,' she supplied, before I could. She'd done her homework.

Not that we thought of Tyler in that way any more. He was our permanent foster child these days, and just as he

2

called us mum and dad, so the 'foster' tag had long since disappeared from the 'son' bit, at least in our heads.

With football training in the morning, Tyler was already up in his bedroom, having just gone up to catch up with one of his favourite crime programmes on his new laptop – the surprise sixteenth birthday present we'd presented him a couple of weeks back. To say he was pleased would be the understatement of the year. If not the century.

But it looked like our own viewing plans were about to be scuppered, EDT being short for emergency duty team, the go-to people for any child who was placed into local authority care out of office hours.

Not that this child – or rather teenager – had just come into care. Helena Curry went on to explain that the girl, whose name was Keeley and who was fifteen years old, had actually been in care since she was ten. 'She's run away from her foster family, basically,' she said. Her voice sounded tired. 'Was picked up by the police a couple of hours ago.'

'Oh dear,' I said, imagining this most complicated of scenarios. It was dispiriting enough when a child entered the system in the first place, but there was an added sadness when a child was already in the system – particularly if they'd been in care long term. You tried to stay optimistic but experience had long since shown me that a downward spiral could so easily happen.

'I know,' Helena agreed. 'She refused point blank to return, and when they tried to insist she made quite a serious allegation against the male carer. So here we are. In need of alternative accommodation – and with specialist carers, which you and your husband, of course, are.'

'Ah,' I said, trying to work out what this might mean for us. 'So it wasn't just a case of fetching up at W for Watson, then?'

She laughed. 'Not in this case, no. No, given the circumstances, and the length of time the girl has been in care …' There was a pause. It felt a pregnant one. 'And from what's on her file …'

I was impressed. This was what should always happen, obviously, when emergency carers were sought, but, in my experience, often wasn't the case. 'So, just temporarily?' I asked.

'In the first instance, yes. Just for the weekend. Though you don't need me to tell you, assuming she's *not* going back, that specialist carers such as yourselves will be sought. So …'

'So she could be our next long-term placement,' I finished for her.

'Exactly,' she said. 'So, are you happy to take her?'

'Yes, of course,' I said, looking at Mike for a confirm-atory nod. Which he gave. We'd been talking about our next placement only the other day; as in who, and most importantly, *when* it might be. With the school summer holidays done with, I was getting itchy fostering feet. 'I'll call my link worker and leave a voicemail for him to ring me in the morning. What time were you thinking of?' I added, glancing at the clock on the mantelpiece. It was already nearly a quarter to eleven.

Helena explained that Keeley was still with the police, but they were ready and waiting to take her anywhere it was decided she was going to go. 'Certainly within the hour, I'd say,' she finished.

'And do you have any more you can tell me now?' I asked, thinking about the file she'd already alluded to.

'Lots, I imagine, but not right now,' she said. 'Can I call you back once I've been back to the police and told them what's happening? Give me a chance to have a skim through and see what might be useful.'

I told her I'd appreciate it – information is power, after all – and she promised she'd call back as soon as she could and, if that proved impossible, that she'd call again first thing in the morning. 'Sorry to interrupt your evening,' she finished. 'Hope you weren't in the middle of anything important.'

Mike had un-paused the telly while we'd been talking, in favour of recording it for later, so I was able to watch James McAvoy smile disarmingly as he took his seat on the famous sofa. Smiling – I swear – right at me. No, not important at all, I thought, as I said goodbye and pushed my mobile into my pocket, before briefing Mike on the few details he hadn't already picked up.

'So come on then, kiddo,' I said to him, pulling on his arm. 'We have work to do upstairs before she gets here. If you can drag yourself away from this, that is.'

Mike groaned. '*Work*? What kind of work? It's nearly eleven o'clock at night, love. You can't seriously be considering a spring bloody clean. It's pink, so as far as I'm concerned it's fine as it is.'

Which it was, more or less. And this being a girl was handy. Our third long-term girl placement in a row, as it happened. Well, bar a couple of short stays, of course. And yes, perhaps a bit *too* pink – it was as pink as it was plastered in butterflies and flowers – but no, it didn't really need anything doing to it. Bar the usual.

'I *obviously* don't mean the whole change-the-décor thing,' I told him. 'But I'll still have to have a dust and freshen up in there. It'll be stuffy. Come on! James'll have to wait.'

'And what about her?' Mike asked as he got to his feet. 'Any inklings of what we might expect?'

'Not as yet,' I said. 'Like I said, the woman's going to call me back.'

'But what's your gut instinct?' he said, as he followed me into the kitchen.

'I'm not sure,' I said, as I rooted in the cleaning cupboard. 'We'll see soon enough.'

I handed Mike the air freshener and polish.

Trouble. The word sprang to mind then. I expected trouble. She was fifteen and had made a serious allegation against a male carer. However that panned out, whether it was substantiated or otherwise, there would be trouble aplenty, and for all concerned.

I handed Mike a duster. And kept my thoughts to myself.

Within half an hour the spare room was suitably freshened and, with the addition of the fairy lights Mike had wound through the headboard of the bed, looked positively cheerful.

I sent him off to update Tyler – assuming he wasn't already asleep – and tell him we could do all the meet-and-greet stuff in the morning.

'Lovely!' I said to myself, feeling my usual prickle of anticipation. A quick whizz round downstairs and we'd be ready to receive our visitor.

'And put the kettle on!' Mike whispered, following me from the landing as I headed down the stairs. 'It's probably going to be a long night and I'm going to need coffee.'

'Not necessarily,' I said, as we regrouped in the kitchen. 'The poor girl is probably exhausted and just wants her bed.'

'So say you,' Mike said. 'She might not even want to be brought here. Out of the frying pan and all that ...'

I sprayed some air freshener on the kitchen counter. 'And into our delightfully fragrant and lovely home.'

By the police. Which was a second thought that struck me, and wasn't wonderful. As foster carers we had to be ever sensitive to the fact that we weren't necessarily the most popular of neighbours. Indeed, in our former home, if not exactly hounded out, we had been at one point the subject of a petition urging us to move, after a child in our care went on a neighbourhood nicking spree. And the sight of police cars outside this house never went down terribly well either. Much less the armoured security van that had famously delivered one boy a while back.

But, with any luck, our latest charge would be delivered more discreetly and not give cause for any tongues to start wagging.

But it wasn't our night for that kind of luck. Within the hour, as Helena had promised (though, sadly, before the promised phone call), there was an enormous squad car pulling up outside the house. It was definitely a proper, full-blown police car.

No sirens, thank goodness, but, under the glow of the streetlamps – not to mention our neighbour's carriage lamps – it was about as inconspicuous as a polar bear.

'Trouble,' Mike said, coming up behind me at the window. 'Seriously. I can feel it in my bones.'

Chapter 2

The car stopped and I let go of the living-room curtain. So once again we were going in cold. Which was a far cry from the way it had been when we started. And, from what I heard from other foster carers, that seemed to be increasingly the case.

With our first foster child, Justin, the placement had been a staged process. First an initial meeting, then another, to make sure the match was right, then, finally, after some thinking time on both sides, he moved in. Sight-unseen placements were then something of a rarity. But ever since then, it seemed, the balance had been shifting, as more and more children were coming into care in emergency situations, leaving no time for any of the normal preliminaries. Instead, like tonight, it was more often than not a case of 'will you take them?' And if the answer was yes, there they were.

Not that it was quite like that with Keeley. She had a file; I'd just yet to see it. But I wondered if, actually, it really mattered anyway. It might to some, I supposed, but since our whole speciality was to try and successfully foster the unfosterable, it wasn't like we were going to say no, was it? Whatever horrors lurked in their files. And if we took a child *in extremis*, even if it was supposed to be temporary, how could we then send them on their way? Come one, come all. That was us.

Hmm, I thought, perhaps that was why we got called …

'Squad car no less,' I said to Mike.

'See?' he said. 'Trouble.'

'Love, I don't think it being a squad car has any of those kinds of implications. It was probably just the first car they had to hand. Anyway, come on, let's get the door open, shall we?'

By the time we were on the doorstep, they'd emerged from the car. An older male constable, a younger female PC and Keeley herself, who appeared to be laughing at something the latter had just said. So that was something. At least she wasn't too traumatised.

The female officer stuck a hand out as they reached us. 'Hi,' she said brightly. 'I have one Keeley McAlister for you. I gather you're expecting her?'

The girl had stopped laughing now, returning my smile with her best sullen expression – the kind I'd seen many times before. Just as teachers were always instructed not to smile before Christmas, so some kids in care, particularly if they've been in care a while, adopt a 'whatever' look as a shield.

I ignored it. 'Hello, love,' I said, as brightly as the policewoman. 'I'm Casey, and this is Mike.' Mike smiled too.

'Come on through,' I went on. 'It's getting a bit nippy out there, isn't it?'

'Not according to young Keeley here,' the male officer told us as they trooped one by one into the living room. 'She doesn't feel the cold, do you, love? Not even after walking twenty-five miles.' He grinned. 'It *was* twenty-five miles, you walked, wasn't it, love?'

I followed the policeman's smiling gaze, taking Keeley in properly. She was a good-looking girl, with thick, glossy hair, which was conker-coloured and tied back in a neat ponytail. And she was clearly well looked after, at least in all the practical ways; wearing very expensive trainers – clean, just like the rest of her – below a pair of high-end labelled tracksuit bottoms and zip-up hoody.

Taking my cue from the officer, who was clearly gently ribbing her, I widened my eyes. 'Twenty-five miles!' I gasped. 'My God, you must be exhausted! Did you get lost?'

Keeley turned to me, now adopting an impressive look of condescension. 'I didn't get *lost*,' she drawled. 'I knew exactly what I was doing. I was just trying to put a bit of distance between me and "home".' She raised her hands and did the quote marks with her fingers. Her nails were perfectly manicured and painted in blood-red polish. 'It's not my fault that these lot are a bit slow in locating missing kids, is it? Thought I was gonna have to walk around all night.'

'Um, excuse me, young lady,' the female officer said, stepping forward. 'I think you'll find you were located half an hour after you were reported missing. Your foster carers had no idea you *were* missing at first, did they?'

'Pft!' Keeley hissed, swinging her ponytail for effect. 'By foster carers you mean Zoe and her paedo husband, I guess? I'm surprised they didn't just leave me to rot.'

Mike and I exchanged a glance, then we both looked at the police officers. Since they'd liaised with all parties concerned, I presumed they'd have something to add.

The female PC duly flipped open her notebook. 'As I think you've been told, Mr and Mrs Watson, Keeley has made an allegation about her foster dad, and that will have to be investigated, of course. But in the meantime she doesn't want to go back, and the carers have said they are happy with that.' She looked at Keeley. 'They also, under-standably, feel the placement is at its end. No going back. Anyway, that's obviously for social services to discuss with you after the weekend. In the meantime, as I say, we'll be looking into the allegations.'

I looked at Keeley too, wondering exactly what had happened. If, indeed, anything had. She was busy stifling a yawn. But then perhaps she was exhausted. Whatever else was true, it had probably been a very long day for her. The dark smudges under her eyes weren't just make-up. She was also shifting from hip to hip and I could tell from her posture that the oversized handbag hanging from her shoulder was probably very heavy.

I pointed towards it. 'Is that all you have with you, love?' I asked.

Children usually came with a suitcase or something similar. Even the most neglected kids we'd ever seen had come accompanied by a bag of rags. But Keeley obviously hadn't packed. She presumably had only what she'd gone out with. Had this been an impulsive decision?

Keeley yawned now, and as she was doing so she nodded. 'Got my toothbrush and PJs,' she said, 'and my phone and my charger. Would it be okay if I go to bed now? I'm knackered.'

I nodded. 'Yes, course you can, love,' I said. 'You must be very *tired*,' I then added, considering and deciding against pulling her up on her own choice of word. 'Come on, I'll show you to your room and leave you to get ready for bed, then I'll bring you up a drink and some biscuits, if you like. I imagine you're hungry. Actually, would you prefer a sandwich?'

Keeley shook her head. 'A drink and biscuits will be fine, thanks.' She then followed me out of the room, without another word to anyone, much less a thank you for the police officers who'd been her taxi for the evening. They shrugged at her departing back. They'd dealt with worse.

'Any other kids live here?' she asked, as I followed her up the stairs.

I nodded as she turned on the landing. 'Here you go, love,' I said, pushing the door to the spare room open. 'And yes, we have a boy. He's called Tyler. He's sixteen – but only just. So maybe the same school year as you? Anyway, you'll meet him in the morning. He's asleep now, I think.' Which made something else occur to me. 'Were there other children at your last placement, love?'

I'd registered Keeley's sour expression when I mentioned the word 'school', but now it changed again.

She looked emotional suddenly. She nodded. 'Yes, my foster sister, Jade. She's fourteen.'

'And they foster her too?' I asked, my mind chugging. An allegation against their foster father might well change that.

But Keeley shook her head. 'No. She's adopted. They adopted her when she was little.' Her face fell, and she suddenly looked younger than before. 'I'm going to miss her. Not them two, but I'm going to miss Jade, big time.' She met my eye then. 'She was like my real sister, you know?'

I smiled sympathetically, and told her I did know. 'And I'm sure you'll see her again,' I said, reaching out to squeeze her shoulder. She was a good three or four inches taller than me. Which, admittedly, wasn't hard. 'Now, you get yourself settled.' I pointed across the landing. 'There's the bathroom, obviously. I'll just go downstairs and finish up with the police then I'll be back with your drink, sweetie, okay?'

'I wouldn't count on it,' Keeley said.

I was confused. 'Count on what?'

'On me being able to see her. I've got four *actual* brothers and sisters. Did they tell you that? I bet they didn't. I've never seen any of them since the day I went into care. Not even once. Social services are all bastards.'

Four. Never seen again. My heart wept for her. But now I had to speak. Start as you mean to go on and all that. Especially with a kid that's been in the system a long time. 'Sweetheart, I know you're angry, and you've every reason to be,' I said gently. 'And we will sit down and talk about all this, I promise. But we don't allow that kind of language here, okay? Me and Mike have young grandkids, so it's just one of our rules. One of our *few* rules. So can you try to think of other words you can use?'

She had the grace to look embarrassed, which surprised me. From her initial demeanour, I'd been expecting more attitude. I wouldn't have been surprised if she'd answered with 'whatever'. Or told me to sod off and leave her alone. So though it was only a small thing it was an important one; it built a bridge between us. 'Sorry,' she said, looking downcast. 'I'll try not to.'

'Thank you,' I said. 'I know you will.'

The consensus wasn't quite so positive when I returned to the living room. 'Yes,' the female officer was saying, presumably in answer to something Mike had asked her, 'we do think the accusation against Mr Burke is probably false. It just came out of nowhere, for one thing, and was quite a time coming. We were asking her why she didn't want to go back there, obviously, and she was coming up with all kinds of reasons for running away. They were too strict, too fussy, too stupid and so on. The usual teenage things you'd expect. And, of course, at that point there was no question that we wouldn't be taking her home again. Of course we would be. But when we explained that – that we had no choice but to do that – out the accusation suddenly came. With a smirk, even, like she knew exactly what she was doing. "Steve's been touching me up," she goes. "There! You can't take me back now, can you?"' The policewoman flipped the cover of her pad back. 'And she's right, of course. We have to act on the allegation. But we aren't convinced there's any truth in it. Not as yet.'

Even though I'd had my own suspicions about the veracity of Keeley's allegation, I was still a bit stunned. Would a fifteen-year-old really be so bad that she would make up something so horrible, and even *smirk* about it? I knew the answer, of course, because I wasn't born yesterday. And as foster carers, Mike and I heard about things like this all the time. Well, if not all the time, at least often enough to scare us, because it was a situation we could potentially find ourselves in. It didn't bear thinking about.

I shook my head, said my farewells and, while Mike showed them out, went into the kitchen to pour a glass of milk and find some Jaffa Cakes.

Then I went back upstairs with them (Mike was still on the doorstep, talking about the engines in squad cars – at this time?) and pushed the slightly ajar bedroom door open with my foot.

'Here you go, love,' I said as I entered.

Keeley, already in bed, yanked the duvet up to her chest. 'Don't we have rules about knocking?' she asked. She also blushed, instantly and furiously.

I could have kicked myself. And now I felt my cheeks flush as well. 'I'm sorry, love,' I said, placing the drinks and snack down on the bedside table. 'Of course we do. I should have knocked. I'm just tired as well, I suppose. And I didn't think you'd be so quick getting yourself into bed.' I smiled apologetically. 'Next time, I will knock. I promise.'

'It's okay,' Keeley said. She raised a hand holding a smartphone. 'I just wondered. Could I have your wifi password, please? I just want to drop a message to my foster

16

sister. You know, to let her know I'm okay and that. I won't phone her,' she added meekly. 'I know it's late.'

I could hardly say no. It was a reasonable enough request. The girl was fifteen and how many of those *didn't* have a smartphone? And it made perfect sense that she'd want to tell the one person she obviously felt close to that she was okay. I recited the password – long since memorised from having to constantly give it to the grandkids and other guests – and once she'd typed it in and got connected I went back downstairs.

'She's online,' I told Mike once we were back on the sofa. It was very late but, despite what I'd told Keeley, I now felt wide awake.

'So all's well with the world,' he said, rolling his eyes. 'Spot of James McAvoy, then?'

I was just opening my mouth to share my joy at that prospect, when my own smartphone buzzed, with no caller ID, which I knew meant the lady from EDT again.

Mike put down the remote he had only just picked up. Yes, it was late, but if there *was* trouble ahead, we might as well know where it was coming from.

Chapter 3

It turned out to be a very long night. Not because Keeley herself gave us any problems, and not because I watched *The Jonathan Ross Show* seven times. Simply because I was on the phone to Helena Curry for the best part of an hour, and then had to relate everything she'd told me to Mike. No, we might not have had a meeting, but it felt almost as good as, because she was having a quiet night, had most of the file and was happy to chat.

Our conversation wasn't an edifying one. As Keeley had already told us, she was indeed one of five siblings. The oldest of them, in fact, by some distance. She'd been ten when they'd been taken from their heroin addict mother, the other four ranging in age from six down to just four months old. It seemed that Keeley had been their primary carer.

Their only carer, at the end. The poor, poor child.

There had apparently never been any father on the horizon, Helena also confirmed – though that didn't particularly surprise me. The mother hadn't even come up with any father's name (refused to, apparently) so it wasn't even clear if the siblings shared full DNA.

Keeley's mother's world was one with which I was rather too familiar. It was one in which having babies wasn't something planned – just an inconvenient by-product of being off your face on drugs every day. And it often wasn't just drug-fuelled abandon, either. It was something women often had to do to keep their drug-dealers – their drug lifeline – sweet. And, as with any world run by ruthless dictators, which the drug world definitely was, there were no safety nets for those at the bottom of the heap, much less family planning guidance or contraception.

Keeley's family had had a long history with social services. They had been known to them for several years before the children were actually taken, as is often the case. I could all too easily envisage the endless cycle of visits and recommendations, of promises made and broken, of 'at risk' children see-sawing between their mother's desperate attempts to get clean, and then failing, and the inevitable neglect. The measures social services would implement would become ever more intense, then, till the point where it would be unconscionable, if not indefensible, to let the children remain in the family home.

I wondered where and how the mother was now. Whether she was still alive even. Chances were she might not be. There was nothing on the file to say either way, apparently. In any event it was an everyday tragedy. Her life had already been that, whatever had happened to her subsequently. Five children existed, without her, to prove it.

And however much I could sympathise with the mother (heroin is a horrible addiction) my greatest sadness was for her children. And, more than that, for the fact that they'd been separated. Helena wasn't sure about the whys and wherefores of that, because it had all obviously been a long time ago. All she knew was that the children had all been taken one night, following a tip-off from a neighbour about hearing screams and shouts, and that when the police and social services had attended the incident a man known to the police – a local drug dealer, Helena read out – had been arrested and charged with several offences.

The children had been scattered pretty quickly. Keeley went to one foster family, the two next oldest to another, while the little ones, as was usual in cases like these, went to a further home and were both immediately put up for adoption. 'It looks like the middle two are still with the same foster family,' Helena told me. 'And it says here that the youngest went to adoptive homes pretty quickly. Or even home singular. They might have gone together, mightn't they? Either way, I doubt there'll be any more to know about them now.'

But what of Keeley? Why no happy ever after for her? And how must have it felt to be wrenched away from them all? I couldn't quite get my head around how devastating that must have been for her, particularly if, as Helena said, she'd been so responsible for their welfare. How on earth must she have processed such a horrendous trauma? One minute being a second mummy to four cherished younger siblings, the next being cast adrift and denied any contact.

How could she possibly come to terms with being allowed no contact with the brothers and sisters she had looked after since they had been born?

'I honestly can't understand it,' I said to Mike as we chatted on into the not-so-small hours. '*Surely* it would have been better to allow them to see each other. Better for all of them, too – not just Keeley. That must have been terrible for them. It's borderline barbaric. Maybe not so much the baby, bless him, but for the others … I just can't believe they'd *do* that. It honestly beggars belief.'

I had, of course, raised the question with Helena. I'd had personal experience of children being denied access to one another, after all. In that case because the older child, who'd been horribly abused sexually, had started behaving inappropriately towards their sibling because they didn't know any different.

But this didn't appear to be the case with Keeley, who'd apparently done her best – at least as far as what Helena knew of the record went. But decisions sometimes get made based on instinct and experience as much as anything. But whatever the full picture, Keeley's care for her little brothers and sisters had been repaid by being taken away from them. That's how it must have seemed to her. No wonder she hated social services.

'They *must* have had their reasons,' Mike said. 'And don't forget, that's often how it goes with long-term fostering and adoption. Maybe for the new families – the ones who ended up with the others, that is – it was part of the deal. A complete new start, with no reminders of or links to the past. Maybe that was it? To give the best chance for four, at the expense of one? These must be hard choices to have to make.'

'But should they even be allowed to stipulate that? I mean, why would knowledge of an older sister hurt a child? Surely it would be a comfort to them to know they had blood family to call their own?'

'Or maybe, given how little they were, it was decided it would be less complicated for them psychologically, easier for the parents, not having the spectre of a complicated older sister, social services involved in their lives, and –'

'But what about Keeley? What about *her* happiness? It just seems so wrong.'

Mike touched my arm. I was raising my voice now. 'How do we know they didn't think it best for Keeley too? I know it seems insane to you now, but maybe at the time they felt she'd become too much the carer –'

'But to deny all contact – *why*?'

Mike shrugged. 'Love, I honestly don't know. But what I do know is that we don't live in a perfect world. You of *all* people should know that.'

I did know that, and maybe he was right, but still my heart ached for the poor kid. She'd been removed from everything she knew, and the siblings she loved, and was now just another kid in care, forgotten by wider society, and, after five long years, was deeply embedded in the system. How heavy must be the emotional weight she carried. And none of it her fault.

Most depressing, however, was the knowledge that her placement with the Burkes must have felt like the best outcome imaginable. She'd been placed with emergency carers first, where she'd spent a wretched few weeks, by all accounts. Thrown into emotional chaos, she'd apparently been described as a 'nightmare'. Then moved on, to an interim placement, with specialists like we were, before the Burkes, who fostered for the same county council, said they'd be happy to take her in long term.

'To complete the adoption illusion for them too,' I said to Mike, my voice bitter on the poor girl's behalf. 'Helena read me a little bit of a looked-after child review she had. You know, Keeley actually said that she felt she had been brought in as a playmate for Jade – can you imagine that? How it must have felt? To fill the gap as the couple couldn't have children of their own. Like a toy ordered off the flipping internet for their existing child to play with, almost. Well, that's obviously how it felt to Keeley. She said she never felt part of the family, not really. Oh God, Mike, what must her mind be *like*?'

'I don't know, Casey,' Mike said, 'but I have a feeling we'll probably find out pretty soon, don't you?'

And that had been his last word on the subject. And, after finally dropping off at around four in the morning, he was already gone from the bed when I woke up. Which didn't surprise me that much – Mike was an early riser both of necessity and by choice. He managed a big warehouse, and it was physically demanding work. He'd have to catch up with a power nap on the sofa later.

As would I, I thought, yawning as I pulled on my dressing gown. Well, if I was allowed the opportunity.

Casey Watson

I crept out of the room and tiptoed downstairs, so as not to disturb either Tyler or Keeley, and eventually found Mike out having a coffee in the back garden. I pulled my dressing gown closer, feeling the nip in the morning air, glancing up at the sky and squinting at the brightness.

'I see you've found the only sunny patch left to sit in,' I said, pulling out one of the cold, plastic chairs, and checking it for cobwebs. For all its beauty, autumn was a horribly spidery time of year. 'Looks like it'll be a nice day, doesn't it?'

'Seems that way,' Mike said, looking up at the sun as well. 'But let's cross our fingers that we don't have a storm to contend with in the house instead.'

I sipped my coffee, enjoying the warmth on my face, as we sat and chatted through our thoughts following the previous night's revelations, and, in my case, observing that a fine sunny morning always made everything seem so much easier and nicer. Because, despite my sulks, I did enjoy the garden at this time of year. Not least because we still had lots of flowers in bloom, but the wasps had mostly buggered off to wherever it was they went in the winter, so I could enjoy it without being dive-bombed.

'All may be well,' I said resolutely. If my night-time reflections achieved one thing, it was a much more positive mindset. Now I knew what Keeley had been through I was even more determined to do my best for her, however much teenage attitude she might sling my way. And, right now, her behaviour had only been as expected. She was fifteen. She knew her stuff. She was a child of the system. Nothing I couldn't deal with standing on my head.

24

I was about to say so when Mike nudged me and mouthed 'shush'. I followed his gaze. 'Would you look at that?' he said, grinning.

Both Tyler and Keeley were standing at the kitchen sink, and it appeared they were already chatting away to each other. They certainly weren't looking out, seeing us looking in.

'That's nice,' I said. 'Nice to see them chatting already.'

'No, but, Tyler? Up willingly? Before half eight on a Sunday morning? Incredible. Come on,' he said, rising. 'Let's go and join the party, shall we?'

Which was a cereal party apparently. Tyler had the cupboard open and was bent down running through the various options.

'Hello you two,' I said, as Mike and I joined them. 'You're both up bright and early for a Sunday. Did a bomb go off upstairs or something?'

Tyler had something of a self-conscious look about him, I decided. But then, Keeley, in her nightwear, was quite an arresting sight.

'Oh, morning, Mum,' he said. Then, glancing at Keeley, 'We just met on the landing, both wanting to use the bathroom. So I thought I'd come down and show her where everything was and that.'

'Yeah, awks or what?' Keeley added brightly, grinning at him. She looked like she'd slept well, at least. 'I'm just going to have some breakfast if that's okay – I'm *starving* – before I get dressed and stuff. By the way, have the social given you any spends for me yet? I'm going to need some new clothes. Apart from some bits, I've only got what I had on yesterday.'

I took in 'bits' – by which I presume she meant undies – and also took in the way she clearly knew all about the financial arrangements that social services would put in place.

But not yet. 'No, they haven't, I'm afraid,' I said. 'And I doubt they will yet, either. In fact, a social worker will probably go and collect your things from home for you, and bring them here – well, assuming you're still not going back home.'

Keeley made a kind of snorting sound. 'It's not home,' she answered, reaching to take her chosen cereal from the cupboard. 'And like I was just saying to Tyler, I wouldn't hold my breath, Katy. Zoe and Steve have probably already put my stuff out for the bin men. They'll have done it as soon as they knew I wasn't coming back. That's what they're like.'

'Casey,' Mike corrected her. 'It's Casey, not Katy.'

'Oh, sorry,' she said, having the grace to look abashed.

'No matter,' I said. 'Lots to take in last night, and you were tired. Anyway, I'm sure that won't have been the case, but let's see what happens tomorrow, eh? Who is your social worker, by the way? Might be someone I know.'

'Danny,' she said. 'Danny Kemp?'

I didn't know of him. I said so.

'He's quite new? Maybe that's it. He's only been my social worker for a few months. He's really nice, he is.' She glanced at Tyler again. 'Not like my last one. She was a right bitch.'

I raised my brows. 'What, bitch?' Keeley said immediately. 'Is that a swear word here? *Really*?'

I could see Tyler smirking out of the corner of my eye, so I glared at him. I could read him like a book. He could see she was going to be good value for money. 'Swear word or not, it's not appropriate, love, okay? So I'd just rather you didn't. Anyway, I said,' reaching up for bowls for the pair of them. 'Why don't the pair of you pour your cereal and take it into the other room, so you can watch a bit of telly while I make something cooked, yes?'

They did as instructed and soon trotted off into the living room. 'So, what d'you reckon?' Mike whispered once they'd gone. 'Storm force ten? Or just a squall, you think? She's certainly got some attitude.'

Entirely expected for a child of the system. 'Persistent drizzle,' I decided upon. 'Nothing I can't handle.'

But it was something that looked like I'd be handling on a fairly regular basis, if the events of the morning were anything to go by.

Having had a breakfast of the cereal, followed by an egg and bacon sandwich, Keeley disappeared upstairs to wash and dress, only to come back down three-quarters of an hour later completely transformed. That handbag of hers must have been from the same place as Mary Poppins got hers from, I decided, if the amount of make-up she'd applied was anything to go by. She waltzed into the kitchen while I was sorting out a pile of washing, with perfectly drawn-on eyebrows, a set of spider-like fake lashes and a generous slick of gothic grey eyeshadow. Foundation and blusher – lots of both – competed for attention with a deep and disarming red lipstick.

Mike and Tyler, both about to set off themselves, to watch Kieron playing football, had painted faces too – with a picture of shock and, in Tyler's case, awe. I knew my husband's expression well; had it been Riley standing there, aged fifteen, it would have been the precursor to him demanding that she wash it off immediately, with his usual 'You are not leaving this house looking like that!'

He didn't, though, and I stepped in before he *did* say it, with, 'You look nice, love,' followed by what I thought was a reasonable enough comment that she might perhaps want to save such dramatic make-up for when she was off out somewhere.

'I *am* going out,' she said, with a 'what of it?' kind of expression. 'So, do I have a coming-in time?' then the barest pause. 'Don't forget, I'm nearly sixteen.'

A child of the system, I reminded myself. Even though I was pretty gobsmacked. 'Keeley,' I answered nicely, 'it would be polite to ask if you can go out, love. Not just announce that you are. Where are you going, anyway?'

Keeley, who'd grabbed her hoody off the newel post and was busy pulling it on, pulled a face and neatly side-stepped the question. 'Well, I'm allowed, aren't I? I know my rights. I didn't realise I had to ask. Not at my age. I can go out unaccompanied so long as I'm in at a reasonable time. I *am* being polite – by asking what time I have to be back.' She looked from me to Mike. Tyler just gawped. 'So, what do you think a reasonable time *is*? I didn't realise I had to tell you my itinerary.'

Oh, so this was how it was going to be, was it? The tension was suddenly almost palpable. And now Mike did speak. 'Excuse me, young lady,' he said. 'Casey was being perfectly reasonable in asking you where you are going. We also have rights,' he added. 'Which are also very reasonable. One of which is knowing where our foster children are when not in the house.'

Another face and now a head shake. 'God!' she huffed. 'I'm just off to meet mates, that's all. I won't be late and Tyler has my phone number if you want it.' Oh, really? Already? 'I just need my pocket money, *please*, because there's stuff I need to buy. Cigarette filters and papers,' she added, as if further keen to challenge us. 'Is *that* all right?'

Despite everything I'd reminded myself about Keeley's awful background, I was only human, and felt suddenly livid. But recognising that had been entirely her intention, and that this was just the first step in a process that would involve lots of boundary realignments, I picked up my handbag, found my purse and passed Keeley five pounds. 'There you go,' I said, 'but you should know that you can't smoke here, at our house, and that tea will be at six. It's entirely up to you whether you want to come back and eat with us, but that's the time the food will be out, okay? And if you don't want to eat – and, again, that's your choice, love – then we'd like you to be no later than nine o'clock tonight. I think that's fair for someone of your age. Is that okay?'

Mike and Tyler were now staring at me as though I'd lost the plot, but Keeley, nodding, took the fiver, stuffed it in her own bag, and made for the front door. Then, as an afterthought – to wind me up a little further, I imagined – she turned back again. 'I don't suppose you have a spare bottle of wine I could take with me?'

Mike spluttered into his coffee mug. Actually spluttered, spraying liquid out of the top of it. 'Afraid not, love,' I said nicely. 'We're all out.'

'Oh. My. God.' Tyler said, hauling his jaw up as soon as the front door banged shut. 'Is she for *real*?'

'It's all bravado, love,' I said, conscious that my pulse was thumping in my temples. 'She's just trying to shock us. Just testing the water. She'll soon settle down.'

Mike ran a hand through his hair. 'I hope you're right,' he said. 'I'm starting to hope it's all a big mistake and that her usual carers will ask for her to be sent back home.'

'I don't think that's going to happen somehow,' I said, looking towards the hall she'd just swept down, and imagining her strutting off down the road, trying to work out who'd won the first round. Did she even know where she was? Have any idea where she should be heading? 'I have a feeling that this might just be the start of quite a long journey.'

Tyler still looked aghast. 'Mum, was I like that when I came here? She's so cheeky!'

'No,' I said. 'Well, a bit. But don't you worry. Not for long!'

Though with a good deal more confidence than I felt.

Chapter 4

Keeley arrived home just as I was dishing up our roast dinner, so I assumed she must have been hungry. We'd normally have had it at lunchtime, but with the weather having been so nice it made sense to move it along to early evening. And I was glad I had, because Keeley sniffed the air appreciatively as she unzipped and took off her hoody.

'Perfect timing,' I said, smiling at her, the morning's tensions forgotten. As I'd intended they should be. Rome wasn't built in a day, after all. (How many times had I told myself *that*, since I'd been fostering, I wondered?) 'Roast chicken,' I went on as she followed me into the kitchen. I gestured towards the pans on the stove and lifted lids in turn. 'Do you like all these vegetables?'

'Yeah,' Keeley said, 'all of them. But not too much gravy, please. Zoe used to drown everything she cooked with the bl— the stuff.'

Progress, I thought. 'Good,' I said. 'Well, off you go to wash your hands – Mike and Tyler are doing likewise, so you'd best nip upstairs. Then straight to the table. I'm about to dish up.'

'I'll do it here,' she said, going to the sink. 'And then I can help you, if you like.'

Well, well, I thought. Progress indeed.

So that's what she did, washing her hands at the kitchen sink and drying them on a clean tea towel. 'What's that?' she asked, nodding towards a misshapen array of coloured lumps on a board on the window sill.

I turned to look. 'Oh, that's just a few of my grand-daughter's salt dough creations. Marley Mae,' I clarified. 'My daughter was over earlier. She's four. Not my daughter,' I said, correcting myself. 'My granddaughter.'

Keeley made a cooing noise as she studied the various creations. 'Ah, that's so sweet,' she said. 'What is it? A sheep or something?'

'I believe that one's a unicorn.' I told her. 'Just a rather short one.'

Keeley laughed as she finished drying her hands. 'Blimey. You don't look old enough to have a grand-daughter,' she said. 'You don't even look as old as Zoe. Are you?'

'I have no idea,' I told her. 'But you're right. I'm not that well preserved – I'm just quite young for a grand-mother, I suppose.'

She smiled. She had a nice smile. It really transformed her face. As was so often the case with teens who made a look of scowling cynicism their default expression. 'Have you any more?' she asked.

'I have four,' I told her as I pulled the chicken from the

oven. 'The oldest is ten now. Which I can't quite get my head round, to be honest.'

I wondered as I spoke about Zoe Burke and what she might be like. I wondered if they'd adopted their first child because they'd tried for quite a while and failed to have one of their own. It made sense, given Keeley's comment about her probable age. For how long had they tried? I wondered how old they were now.

'Blimey, *ten*?' Keeley said, gaping.

I smiled. 'My daughter started very early.'

'And you've got a son as well, haven't you? I mean, as well as Tyler. He told me. Sorry, I'm not being much help, am I? What can I do?'

'I tell you what,' I said, because my guilty secret was that I preferred dishing up solo. 'How about you take a look at something while I do the dishing up?' I went across to my junk drawer (which of course held the exact opposite; everything in it was indispensable, obviously) and pulled out a much-thumbed pink A4 plastic wallet.

'What's this?' Keeley asked as she took it from me.

'It's the family,' I told her, because that was exactly what it was.

It was a relatively recent thing, the family file, but our fostering agency had encouraged all of us to make one. It was a kind of rogues' gallery, containing mug shots of all the family members foster children who stayed with us might come into contact with, together with names, ranks and serial numbers – well, sort of. It was a good idea, too, because it was a quick way to orient a new house guest – right down to pictures of the house itself (it could be sent out to a prospective new child as well, of course), plus some light-hearted details about the family routines.

'Take a look,' I said. 'And I tell you what, why don't you take it on through. I'm sure Mike and Tyler will be happy to fill in any gaps.'

I smiled as she ambled off into the dining room, file in hand. And leaving me to plate the food up unmolested.

'This is just *so* cool,' Keeley was saying to Tyler when I came through with the plates. 'Your mum and dad are so cool too,' she added, glancing at Mike. 'And so *young*.'

Tyler grinned. 'Oh, they're older than they look, you know.'

Keeley giggled, and I noticed how it made Tyler blush. I made a mental note that I'd definitely have to keep an eye on things in that department. I had never seen the lad go this gaga over a girl before. Well, not that I was aware of. What he got up to when out with his mates might be another matter entirely.

'Less of the "old", mister,' I warned, waving a wooden spoon towards him. 'Or there'll be no breast for you – only the parson's nose!'

Of course, I realised the very second the words had left my mouth how inappropriate they sounded. Tyler now looked mortified, and even more so when Keeley laughed out loud. 'Yeah, Tyler,' she teased, waggling a finger, 'no breast for you!' then, to Mike and my joint mortification, actually jiggled her own pair a little.

Mike stood up, clearing his throat. 'Let me help with the other veg,' he said, whispering 'nice one' as he passed me on the way to the kitchen.

But then, once we'd come back with the rest of the food and I tried to steer the conversation away to other, less inflammatory subjects, I got put in my place as well.

'So,' I said, sitting down, once both plates and veg were on the table, 'what's all this about Zoe's gravy?'

Keeley picked up her cutlery. 'You know, Casey,' she said, 'I know you don't want me to swear, so I'd really rather not talk about them, if that's all right with you. All I can say is that Steve is a twat and Zoe is an idiot for putting up with him.' Her gaze took in all of us. 'There isn't really anything else *to* say.'

Keeley was right, of course. There probably wasn't. Not at the dinner table, with her allegation towards her foster father still hanging in the air. So I decided to leave it and just try to enjoy my meal – get this first day over with as little drama as possible. I also decided, on impulse, to break a bit of a house rule by opening up the double doors from dining to living room so that the television could provide the entertainment rather than me. Which worked well; a repeat showing of *Dancing on Ice* improved the mood no end and we managed to finish up without further incident. The only thing that kept occurring to me was that, after we were all done with tea, would Keeley announce that she was going back out again? And if so, would there be another quibble about coming in on time?

Apparently not. It seemed Keeley was done with socialising for the day. Indeed, no sooner had she helped me with the last of the clearing up (uncomplainingly – another tick) than she announced that she was going to turn in for the night.

'Really?' I said, astonished. 'But it's not even eight o'clock yet.'

'I know,' she said, folding a tea towel and hanging it over the cooker handle. 'But I'm just still so tired.' She yawned extravagantly, but not at all convincingly. 'I did walk for miles, you know, whatever that copper told you.'

'Oh, I'm sure you did, love,' I told her, wondering what she planned on doing once up in her bedroom. Certainly not sleep. Not yet, at least. She was all internet-ed up, after all. 'No, you go on up, get some kip,' I said. 'We'll be having the posse here tomorrow, won't we? So you'll need to have your wits about you.'

She rolled her eyes. 'I'd forgotten that.' I didn't think she had for a minute. 'Anyway, I'll just grab a glass of water, if that's okay. Which cupboard was it where you keep your glasses?' Then she yawned again, so I said good-night, and saw her off up the stairs.

'What do you think?' Mike said, once I'd rejoined him and Tyler back in the living room.

'Rejoining the *real* world, I imagine. As in the one on social media. Connecting with all her virtual friends.'

Oh, if only it had turned out to be that innocent.

By 9 p.m. Mike and Tyler were engrossed in playing on the Xbox – some silly football game that I had to absolutely buy every year or apparently the world would spin off its axis and fly off into deep space. And with Keeley out of the picture for the night (I'd heard her shower earlier but nothing since) I used the time to get the laundry sorted out and iron Tyler's school uniform.

What Keeley had said to me earlier about clothes hadn't
been lost on me. If she was to be staying with us after the
weekend – which she almost certainly was – then I would
need to sort some other clothes out for her by one means
or another. Her 'cool' social worker, Danny, would either
have to go and retrieve her belongings, or I would need to
break into my bank balance. About which I wasn't really
too downhearted. For one thing I knew I'd be reimbursed
for what it cost me, and for another, I'd not been on a
shopping trip in a while, so, even if it wasn't for me, I was
quite looking forward to it. It would also be an opportunity for us to do a bit of girly bonding. Whatever had
happened – and I knew it would be a while before I knew
the whole story – the most important job in the short term
was to get her to a place of emotional stability, settle her
in with us, and some time together on our own, engaged
in normal everyday activities, would be all to the good in
that regard.

That said, Keeley really needed to be in school. Like
Tyler, she was in her GCSE year now, so every day missed
would not only mean vital learning lost; it might also have
a serious effect on her final grades. And though Keeley
had seemed indifferent about it when I'd mentioned it
earlier, I knew she'd need to be enrolled in our local one
without delay. She certainly couldn't make the round trip
to her old one. I wondered if she'd figured that into her
thinking when she'd run away, and run so far.

The last thing ironed, I switched the iron off and piled
everything up to take upstairs. I usually left Tyler's either
in his room or just outside it – he was pretty good at

keeping it straight and putting everything away. All was quiet as I climbed the stairs, and again, when I put Tyler's clothes down on his bed. It was only when I stepped back onto the landing that I heard something.

It was talking, of a kind, though the words were indistinguishable – perhaps she was nattering to her foster sister, or perhaps a friend. She clearly had credit on her phone, or even a contract. I hoped her social worker would let me know about that and, more importantly, what I was expected to do about it.

But when I emerged a second time – from hanging Mike's shirts in our wardrobe – I heard a distinctly odd noise. Call me nosey or intrusive – I like to think 'intuitive' – but it was the kind of noise that, though it was impossible to identify, just made me pause and try and work out what it was. Thus I felt compelled to stop outside Keeley's door and listen harder. And there it came again – breathy, almost a kind of keening. Was she upset? But then I heard something else, which could never be misconstrued – a girlish giggle, followed by, 'No, *you* tell me what *you're* wearing first.'

Stunned, I put my ear against the door, feeling no guilt about eavesdropping. Given the serious nature of the allegations she'd made against her foster carer, I wanted – no, I *needed* – to know what was going on.

And there was soon more to go on, which confirmed my first suspicions. Words that could mean anything but, given the tone in which they were said, could only mean one thing. 'Oh, yeah, yeah,' she simpered. 'I'm doing *exactly* that right now ...'

This was no ordinary conversation. Though my heart sank to realise it, I knew exactly what I was hearing. This was what I knew young people casually referred to as phone sex. I cringed a little. I definitely didn't want to hear any more of it. And the question was, who was she having phone sex with?

A boyfriend? A girlfriend? Or someone more sinister? I thought back to a course I'd been on a few years previously, in which the subject was covered as part of a session on child exploitation. So I had to do something. Take action. I knew that. The question was, what? Keeley didn't exactly sound as if she was being exploited, in terms of being coerced, after all. I really didn't want to burst into the room, but nor could I wait till she had finished whatever it was she was doing. Decided, I knocked sharply on the door.

'Keeley,' I said, walking straight in. No waiting for a summons. 'What are you doing?'

She was fully dressed, thank goodness, borrowed pyjamas in place, putting to bed my fears that something visual was going on. But the shock on her face was clear as day. She ended the call without saying another word. Then anger flushed her features. 'I thought we had a deal about privacy!' she snapped at me, throwing her phone down on the duvet. 'My God! It's like I'm six or something!'

It was all bluster, I knew, designed to divert me. Trying to divert the blame *towards* me.

'Um, excuse me, Keeley, but what do you expect me to do, exactly? I could hear you, from the landing. I could hear every word you were saying. Not to mention everything else.' I placed my hands on my hips and raised my brows, waiting for an answer to my question. Two could play at that game.

She folded her arms across her chest and exhaled sharply, her eyes down. As you might when you knew you were going to have to explain something you wish you didn't need to. To an idiot.

'Come on,' I said. 'Look at me, please, Keeley. I think I have a right to know what it was you were doing. This is my house, and you happen to be in my care. Come on. Tell me what's going on.'

'Duh!' she said. 'If you heard, then you already *know*.' She really was speaking to me as if I was stupid. 'It's just phone sex. It pays better than sexting, okay?'

As if that financial gem was the key bit of information I needed. As if the 'crime' here – and she clearly didn't think anything of it – wasn't that she was fifteen and that it was clearly a paying enterprise, only that it ran the risk of someone overhearing. I truly didn't know quite where to begin with her. She was *fifteen*. This was her version of normal teenage life?

'*Just* phone sex?' I said, trying not to gape at her.

'Yes,' she said, obviously not registering my sarcastic tone. She unfolded her arms and picked the phone up again. 'Look, it pays well, okay?'

'Having phone sex. With strangers?'

'*No.*' She looked irritable. 'Not actually doing *anything*. It's just making noises and pretending, that's all. How else d'you think I can earn any bloody money? Sorry,' she added quickly. 'Earn any money.'

I couldn't quite believe what I was hearing. Not so much what she was saying – I wasn't that naïve – as the unconcerned way in which she said it. Yes, she could obviously see I was shocked and cross, but when it came to the business itself – for it clearly was a business (a cottage industry, even?) – it was as if she didn't really see anything wrong in it.

'So,' I said, when I'd digested this. 'Did you know that boy you were talking to?'

'*Boy?*' Keeley spluttered, not even attempting to hide her amusement. 'That was no boy. For all I know that could have been some dirty old man. Of *course* I don't know them. Why on *earth* would I want to know them? They're filthy twats. *All* men are twats,' she added. 'Everyone knows that.'

Two days she'd been with us, that was all. Just two days. And we were already in territory that would be fraught with complications. Uh-oh. *Here comes trouble*, I thought darkly.

Chapter 5

Monday morning, just as I expected, brought a flurry of phone calls, the first, which came at 8 a.m. on the dot, was from our fostering agency link worker, John Fulshaw.

I was obviously keen to fill him in on the events of the previous evening, which I'd written up in my log but decided not to email him about yet, knowing we'd be able to have a proper chat about it in the morning. Not only that; by the time I'd debriefed Mike (only after Tyler had gone to bed) and completed my log, I was almost dropping with fatigue. And having had so little sleep on Saturday night I got into bed and was asleep within seconds of my head hitting the pillow.

But I held fire. First things first. And John was obviously anxious to cover all the basics.

'Yes, you were the "chosen ones",' he confirmed when I relayed what I'd been told about EDT, presumably after discussion, opting for specialist carers from the outset. 'You know what it's like, Casey – older teenagers are difficult to place at the best of times, even if it's only for a couple of nights. And the fact that she made that allegation against her foster father was always going to make it harder. No one relishes that kind of potential complication, do they? But I knew you two would be able to handle her. Not least because you've been there before.'

We had, too. Our second ever foster child, a well-developed and very deeply damaged adolescent girl called Sophie, had started coming on to Mike and Kieron almost as soon as she'd come to live with us, one morning appearing in our kitchen in just her (black, skimpy, lacy) bra and tiny knickers. So, thrown into the deep end with a situation we'd only up to then discussed theoretically, we'd taken advice, and quickly learned how to protect ourselves, by ensuring she was never on her own in the house with either of them.

'So I'm right in thinking that she is likely to be with us for a while then?' I asked John, already knowing the answer.

'I won't lie,' he said. 'I've had a chance to read the file and speak to EDT, and I imagine so. If you're willing to hang onto her, that is.'

To which he already knew the answer as well. 'Of course we are, John,' I reassured him. 'But if that's the case then there's something you need to know right away.'

'Oh, really? You've had problems already?'

'In a way,' I said. 'Though it's not so much a problem as a revelation. Well, it was definitely a revelation to me, I can tell you. John, what do you know about phone sex?'

He chuckled. 'I'm not entirely sure I know how to answer that! No, seriously, probably about as much as the next man. Or woman, of course,' he added swiftly.

'Well, I know a good bit more than I did about it this time yesterday,' I told him. 'More than I'd *want* to know, to be honest. But it seems our young visitor knows substantially more.'

I explained about my unexpected discovery the previous evening, having already taken myself and my mobile out into the back garden, in case Keeley woke up and came downstairs. 'And there's money involved,' I added. 'She does this for money. There's no official charge (Keeley had been more than happy to discuss all this with me, almost proudly), but the person on the other end of the phone can ask her to text her bank details so that he can send her a "gift".'

'Good lord,' John said, his voice going up in pitch. '*Really?*'

'Really,' I confirmed. 'It's as simple as that. She texts her details, they make the payment, job done. No great fortune – it's just the odd tenner, according to Keeley – sometimes just a fiver, depending on how long they "chat". Or some-times – and this is the bit that really worries me – she's even given men her address so they can send her gifts in the post. Not our address, I hope. She says not.'

'She'd barely have had time!' John said. 'She's only been with you five minutes. Just as well you stumbled upon all this when you did, by the sound of things.'

'But what happens now?' I asked. 'This has got to be illegal, hasn't it? Surely it's exploitation?'

John went silent, presumably processing what I'd told him. 'Yes, you would think so, wouldn't you? But *is* it?' he said finally. 'I'm not so sure. I mean, yes, it's clearly wrong – and I'm with you on the exploitation aspect. But in the eyes of the law, if she's a willing participant … and if they are only talking … well, I'm wondering exactly what laws are being broken here.'

'Are you *kidding* me?' I asked, appalled. Not least because John didn't even appear to be that shocked by my revelations. A bit shocked, yes, but not OMG shocked, as Tyler might say. 'I mean, come on – it's clearly some form of abuse, surely?'

'Well, I'd like to think there might be something, but … well, is it? I tell you what. Leave it with me. I'm going to look into this further and get some guidance about what, if anything, can be done. Though first of all I have to call Keeley's social worker, obviously. Try and arrange a time for the two of us to come out and see you together. Later today, ideally. Would that be all right with you?'

I told John that yes, I'd be around all day, and that I'd appreciate it if he could get out to us as soon as possible – if only to advise me on how to address the situation with Keeley's 'hobby', which, for all I knew, could be carrying on upstairs even as I spoke.

I jumped, startled, as I heard Tyler cough behind me. 'Bloody hell, Ty!' I said, clutching my chest with my free hand while I ended the call. 'You're like a bloody ninja. How long have you been down?'

He was already dressed for school and looked embarrassed. I wondered what, if anything, he'd heard. 'I wasn't being nosey,' he said. 'But is that straight up, Mum? About the phone sex? Flipping hell.'

Too much, then. But I'd already had a hunch he probably knew all about phone sex. Or at least the business of boys and girls 'sexting' each other – it had been all over the tabloids in recent years, after all, more often than not because some poor girl had found her explicit, *private* pictures plastered all over social media, after dumping some low-life of a boyfriend.

I followed him back indoors. 'Flipping *heck*,' I said. 'Flipping heck indeed, love. I wish you hadn't heard that. And it's confidential, obviously. And shouldn't you be getting off to school?'

Tyler had been with us long enough to know all about confidentiality. And also to know when a conversation such as this was effectively over.

He nodded, and reached down for his backpack, which was already propped waiting against the front door. 'I know,' he said, 'but you know, Mum, you shouldn't worry too much. It's the latest craze. A couple of girls in my class even do it.'

My eyes widened in disbelief. '*Really*?' Though I was surprised not so much that they did it, as the fact that it was all discussed so openly between peers.

'Honestly, Mum. *Really*,' he said, dutifully dipping his head and proffering his cheek for his farewell kiss. 'They get perfume and make-up and stuff sent through the post – and then they come in and brag about it. I know – it's mad, isn't it?'

Mad. I wasn't sure that was quite the word I'd use. And I was still stuck at astounded. Was that really what some teenage girls did these days? It beggared belief. Did they think it was normal? Did they think it was moral? And more to the point, were their parents aware of how they came by all the plunder? What had happened to taking a bloody Saturday job in a café or something? What was the world coming to, honestly? I thought of Marley Mae and Dee Dee and the teenage world they'd all too soon grow into. But it was such a horrible, unedifying thought that I resolved not to think about it any more.

The morning wore on, and the not-thinking approach mostly worked, but by eleven it struck me that though Keeley, with her traumatic background, was unlike a majority of teens, in one aspect she was exactly like pretty much every one of them, in that, with no school to attend, she still hadn't surfaced.

And not because she was putting a shift in at her personal cottage industry; I'd been 'just passing' all morning, back and forth across the landing like some deranged stalker, and I hadn't heard a peep from her. I made a mental note that tackling someone about her education must be a priority if she were to be staying with us for any length of time. A girl of her age definitely needed to be in school. And a woman of my age definitely needed her to be in school too.

And right now, it was high time she was up, washed and dressed, not least so she'd be fed and presentable when her social worker came knocking.

I knocked myself and, as before, went straight in. What had happened last night meant any concessions to her privacy would henceforth have to be earned.

'Come on, sleepy head,' I said as her head emerged from under the duvet. 'It's almost lunchtime and this afternoon your social worker is coming, along with my boss and a couple of others, so you need to be up and dressed and ready. Would you like breakfast? Or, more accurately, brunch?'

Keeley groaned and rubbed her eyes. She had very pretty eyes, I decided. Pools for Tyler to drown in? I hoped not. 'Is it late, then?' she said, looking around for her mobile. Which she found, in the bed, as was so often the case. 'I don't usually sleep as late as this,' she said, squinting at it. Then, gathering her thoughts, she pouted. 'I s'pose I'll have to put the same clothes on as yesterday again, won't I?'

'Afraid so,' I said, refusing to feel guilty about that. I'd offered to wash them and to lend her some of my own clothes last night, but she'd declined the former and looked at me as if I was insane re the latter. All part of her mission, no doubt, to get me shopping for her without delay.

But her smile was sweet enough as she pulled herself up in bed properly. 'Okay,' she said. 'I won't be long. I'll be down in ten minutes. And just some tea and toast, please, if that's okay?'

I told her it was and was just heading downstairs when my own mobile phone started ringing again. It was John again, who'd now been in touch with Keeley's social worker, Danny, and was able to confirm that they'd both be with us at one thirty.

'And I've spoken with several colleagues about the phone thing as well.'

'And?'

'And you're not going to like it. Because apparently it's a very grey area. For one thing Keeley is almost sixteen, which makes it extremely difficult to prove coercion. And for another, the fact that this seems to be random people she's phoning – who you say she claims she doesn't know from Adam, that's right, isn't it? – just makes it even *more* difficult. If she doesn't know them, then they probably don't know her either, and may well not even be aware of her age. And even if they were, that too would be difficult to prove. Which means it's almost impossible to address legally, on either count; unless there's a specific complaint, or some evidence that someone is abusing or grooming her, it's just so difficult to prove, full stop.'

'So it's *allowed*, then?' I asked, understanding what he was saying, and processing the reason why, but still feeling completely floored by it all. 'A young girl can actually, within the law, have phone sex with strangers? Who pay her? You're actually telling me this is *legal*?'

'It's not as clear cut as that, Casey,' John explained. 'And I do have people digging around for more information for me, but right now that's all I know for sure. We can discuss it when we come over. Though one bit of good news is that I've spoken to a family liaison officer who works with children who've been groomed, and one thing we can do is have him come with us to talk to her. Keeley might not feel very receptive, but I think it's important that we try. If nothing else to spell out the potential danger she may open herself up to – whether it's online or via the phone – particularly if she is giving out her address in order to receive gifts. That part's very worrying.'

And also practised by girls in Tyler's class, apparently, I mused, having yet another 'what's the world coming to?' moment.

'It is,' I agreed. 'And I'd like that to happen very much.'

'I thought you might,' John said, 'given that it's your security at stake too.'

'Not to mention the fact that we really need to nip this in the bud; I can't have this sort of thing going on under my roof.'

'I'll do that,' John assured me. 'If we can pin one down we'll bring along a community support police officer too, just to reiterate that a criminal offence could be taking place without her even being aware of it.'

That I didn't imagine for a moment. I reckoned Keeley was bright enough to be well aware of the ramifications of everything she did. But it couldn't hurt, and a presence in uniform often had an impact, even to a child who'd been in the system long enough to know how to work it to their advantage. Feeling I'd done all I could do for now, I told John I'd see him later, then got down to the business of making our little entrepreneur her breakfast.

Chapter 6

'Oh *God*,' Keeley groaned. 'I *hate* meetings.'

She'd come downstairs in the ten minutes she'd promised. I was impressed. It was also nice to see the pretty fifteen-year-old beneath the make-up, and I hoped she wouldn't feel the need to slap a load more on after she'd eaten, though with her assessment of her social worker Danny as being so cool, I suspected that I'd probably hope in vain. 'Don't we all, love?' I replied.

She sat down heavily on one of the kitchen chairs and groaned again. 'Well, he just better fetch my stuff, at least. That cow will be wearing all my clothes by now. Bet you anything.'

I eyed the pseudo-sportswear that Keeley had come to us in – and was, of course, still wearing – and though I too hoped that her social worker would be bringing some more clothing, I doubted very much that Zoe Burke would currently be parading around her house in baggy Ellesse bottoms. Let alone any kind of designer hoody. But then, what did I know? I didn't know her, did I?

I rolled my eyes and slid the jar of jam across the table.

'Strawberry jam okay?' I asked. Keeley nodded. 'And don't worry. I reminded John, my link worker, that you needed your own things.'

Keeley bit into her toast with her even white teeth. 'Who else did you say was coming?' she asked, her mouth still full of it.

'A community support officer and some kind of family liaison person,' I said. Her brows drew together. She was obviously perplexed. 'Something like that, anyway,' I added. 'Well, as far as I know. Just to speak with you about how to keep yourself safe while using your phone for … Well, the kind of things that you were doing when I heard you …'

Keeley's lower lip dropped open. '*God*,' she huffed. 'You mean you've grassed me up for that? Why would you *do* that? I wasn't doing anything wrong. I told you!' She glared at me then, her nostrils flaring. 'Why would you *tell* people about that? No wonder I go fucking mad at foster carers!'

I banged my cup of coffee onto the table rather more heavily than I'd intended. 'Please don't use that kind of language in this house, Keeley,' I said firmly. 'You don't hear it from us and I don't want to hear it from you. The reason I told Mr Fulshaw what I did is very simple. I have a duty to do so. It's my *job*. And I'd expect you to know by now that foster carers have to fill in daily sheets recording any incidents, and these get passed on. You might not like it, but it's something we have to do and that's that.'

She was still glaring, so I simply glared back at her. There was nothing to be gained by coming over all apologetic. She knew perfectly well I'd had no choice in the matter. And even if I had done, my glare told her, I'd have reported it anyway. We would care for her whether she liked it or not.

I watched her face go through various changes as she clearly tried to work out whether or not to continue to argue with me. Thankfully she took the sensible option.

'I didn't mean to swear,' she said, readily contrite now she'd registered that I wasn't standing for any nonsense. 'And, okay, fine, then. But I really don't need to speak to those people. I'm not stupid. And I'll stop doing it while I'm here if that's what you want.'

Which seemed all too easy. I didn't doubt saying one thing to her foster carers and doing another was second nature to her. 'Yes,' I said anyway. 'That's definitely what I want, obviously. But "those people" are coming out now anyway, so it won't hurt to listen to what they have to say, will it? Now eat your breakfast and then you can go make your bed, please, if you haven't already. No doubt Danny will want to see where you're sleeping.'

'Yeah, right,' she said with an eye roll. 'To make sure I'm tucked up safe in my winceyette pyjamas, clutching my teddy, like a good little girl. Okay, okay, *sorry*,' she added quickly, raising her palms.

* * *

Keeley might well find the whole idea of the impending meeting tedious in the extreme but she didn't make a fuss and went back up to her room to get ready without any further wisecracks.

And I sympathised, too, despite feeling so irritable with her. She must have sat through so many of them, after all.

It was such a singular situation being a child in long-term care, and having your life pored over and discussed by a series of strangers – not to mention having little power to shape your own destiny. I wondered if she was thinking twice now about taking the action that had brought her to us, and again about whether there was any truth in it. Time would tell, but in the meantime the most pressing thing, it seemed to me, was to head her off from her chosen way of getting herself pocket money. I hoped the professionals coming to see her were good at what they did, because I knew kids like Keeley had a built-in off-switch when being lectured by adults – hardened by life, they tended to think they already knew it all.

I did a lightning clean, and was just peeling off my rubber gloves when I spotted John Fulshaw heading up the front path. He was making slow progress, on account of the brace of enormous suitcases he was lugging.

I went to the front door and opened it just as he lowered them to the ground, puffing. They were clearly as heavy as they looked.

'Seems this young lady here' – he nodded towards Keeley, who had rattled down the stairs and was now standing in the doorway with me – 'has too many things to fit into just one car.' He held his hand out to shake Keeley's. 'Nice to meet you,' he said, grinning. 'I'm Casey's supervising social worker, John. D'you want to nip out and bring in the rest? It's all in the boot. Your social worker's following along with the other lot.'

'Of course,' she said, almost shyly (which I took to be a positive). 'I'll just go up and grab my hoody.'

We both watched Keeley sprint back up the stairs. 'Not quite the live wire I'd been led to expect,' John said, as she disappeared across the landing. He hauled the cases inside and rubbed his hands together. 'Jeez. It's bloody freezing out there.'

I smiled. 'Oh, you ain't seen nothing yet,' I said. '"Live wire" is our Tyler. That girl outsparks live wire by a mile, trust me. Just give her time.'

Keeley trotted back down then, feeding her arms into the sleeves of her hoody as she descended. John raised his car keys, once she'd poked her head up through the neck. 'Can you catch?' he asked. She could. 'There you go, then,' he said. 'There's a couple of boxes in the boot and a bin bag on the back seat. Give me a shout if any of it is too heavy for you.'

'No worries. I'll be fine,' she said brightly.

'So what's her social worker like?' I asked him as Keeley now headed off down the front garden path. 'Danny? Oh, you'll like him. Young lad. Mid-twenties. Though he looks about sixteen. Which doesn't make it easy – particularly with older teenagers, or so I'm told. Specially the girls – they apparently either tend to fall immediately in love with him, or decide he's one of their besties.'

'You're remarkably well informed,' I said, raising my eyebrows. 'And it sounds like a dangerous combination. Which category does he fall into for Keeley? Do you know that as well?'

'I do, as it happens. The latter, apparently. Though it's a love–hate kind of thing. One minute she loves him like a brother, the next she hates him – the usual stuff. I suppose it is what it is. But it's generally a good relationship. He's been with her coming up for a year now.'

'I know,' I said. 'Replacing the "bitch".'

John frowned. 'Yes, by all accounts that wasn't such a great match. But, yes, this one seems to be. So that's a positive.'

It was definitely a positive. A child's relationship with their social worker was a complicated and close one, even more so if the child was in long-term care. They were at the sharp end of the council's role *in loco parentis*, and how well they bonded with their child impacted on everything. Even Tyler, very much part of the Watson family these days, still retained a close attachment to his social worker, Will, and that was exactly as it should be. A network of healthy personal attachments was massively important to any child's well-being, but particularly so when that child had already suffered the loss of the ones many of us took for granted.

Not that there was a blueprint for successfully matching children to social workers. For one thing, it didn't really work like that. Cases came in constantly, staff were in perennially short supply, and who they were given was more often than not simply a case of who was on duty. And the strangest pairings – in terms of age, personality and gender – were often the most successful.

Having left the doorstep to drag Keeley's cases upstairs, John and I were now alerted to Danny's arrival by the sound of laughter as we came back down into the hall. They were both coming up the path now, heavily laden with yet more bags and boxes, and I could see straight away that they were comfortable with each other.

John had been right. Danny definitely looked younger than his years. Maybe not as young as sixteen, but he was definitely youthful, an impression heightened by his skinny jeans and cool trainers, and the way his hair was swept back, in what was currently the fashion – he could have stepped straight from the pages of a fashion magazine. Or maybe auditioned for One Direction.

And there was still stuff to bring in apparently. So introductions were made as I trooped out to help, leaving John to go into the kitchen and put the kettle on.

I was staggered by the amount of possessions Keeley had, if I'm honest: at least eight large boxes, two more suitcases – large ones, again – and a variety of bags stuffed with goodness knew what. Most kids we'd had came with far less than this, but I knew that a child who'd been in the system some time could easily amass a fair bit.

Even so, I couldn't help wonder about the extent of it – even for a modern female teenager. Was the glut of possessions the fruit from her labours on the phone? And if so, how much of it did it mean she'd been doing? No wonder she had no interest in going to school.

It was a question I imagined I might answer in time but for now the main thing was where to put it all.

'I'll do it,' Keeley said, when Danny offered to help her upstairs with it. 'That way you can all get on with talking about me, and I don't have to sit there getting brain-dead.'

It was said with no attitude – just a statement of fact. And, having glanced at Danny, who immediately nodded his approval, I told her that was fine. 'Though only while we go through all the files and so on,' I told her. 'Then you'll have to break off and come down.'

'Good. That should give me at least an hour, then,' she said dryly. Then she grinned at Danny. 'I have a *very* thick file, don't I?'

I told the men to set up at the dining table, while I finished making the tea and coffee, and by the time I'd come back in with the inevitable plate of biscuits both John and Danny had already spread out various clipped-together documents on top of it. Care plans, risk assessments and background information. All the things that should make caring for Keeley a breeze.

Well, in theory.

I was actually happy that Keeley had taken herself off for a bit as reading through the case notes – which made for grim reading, even though I already knew the gist of it – I had loads of questions popping into my head, not least of them being to wonder about her blood family, and what *had* become of all those little brothers and sisters. Even if I couldn't help reunite them, I could at least try to find out they were okay and happy, couldn't I? But that would need to wait. First things first, and the first thing in this case was that Danny and John were both keen to establish whether Mike and I would keep Keeley till she was sixteen and, hopefully, a bit beyond. If at all possible, anyway. It seemed she had very different plans.

'Her birthday is only a matter of weeks, now,' Danny added, as if trying to tempt me.

'I know – she's reminded me several times,' I said, grinning.

He nodded. 'The Big Day. And she's certainly been counting them,' he said. 'And I doubt all this imbroglio will have changed her plans either.'

'What sort of plans?' I said.

'To wave bye-bye to the Burkes. Once she's sixteen she can legally stick the proverbial two fingers up at the system, of course.' His face grew serious. 'She's made it abundantly clear that as soon as that day comes, in her ideal world she's "offskies", as she puts it.'

'Offskies where?' I asked. 'And what's going to happen about school?'

'Offskies not too far away, I hope,' Danny answered. 'Though I'm sad to say that school has become a bit of a lost cause.'

My heart sank. 'But she's only just started year eleven,' I said.

'Or rather, *hasn't* started year eleven,' he corrected. 'She's got a long history as a non-attender. I've been trying my best, but, again, her mind's set.'

'And that's that? There's nothing you can do to convince her otherwise?' I asked, concerned. In our short acquaintance, it seemed to me that a sixteen-year-old Keeley, alone in the world, and out of education as well, was a tragedy waiting to happen. 'Does she already have an assigned "moving on" worker, then?' I asked him, recalibrating my thoughts. She'd obviously been planning to escape for some time, then. 'Does she have a pathway plan?'

These were both things put in place when a child was approaching the time they would officially be leaving care. It usually meant that measures would be taken to ensure continued safety until they could properly look after themselves. It could take the form of finding them supported lodgings, or a flat in a supervised building, or, if they were ready for it, complete independence. It all depended on the individual child. And it definitely didn't generally apply to children who were still almost a full year off normal school-leaving age.

Danny nodded. 'We've started a pathway plan,' he confirmed. He then pointed at the biscuits. 'You mind if I take the Bourbon, John?'

'Consider it yours,' John said.

'Thanks. But we have to move quickly because Keeley is so adamant that, no matter what, she doesn't want us interfering in her life beyond sixteen. And with what's just happened, I don't doubt she means it, too. Of course, we'd rather she stay in foster care for a bit longer –' He glanced at John. 'At least till she has some sort of plan in place. Some idea of what she might do for a job. Or, once she's old enough, a college place. But her mind is pretty set. If we don't work *with* her, she could literally just disappear, couldn't she?' I nodded. She certainly could. 'No, we just have to sell the idea well enough that she accepts that if she works with *us* she can still have her freedom, but with the security of us lot lingering in the not too far background.'

'And you'd like Mike and me to be integral in selling that proposition?' I asked. Both men nodded. And it was certainly different, I had to admit. I'd never been in quite this kind of position before. This was a teenager – a pretty smart one – who believed that she didn't need help. She didn't want to be fostered. She didn't want anyone telling her how to live her life any more. And, though she didn't know it, what she'd get, as a result of what she wanted, would be to become just another dispiriting statistic – a child from the care system, lost first in it and then to it. And her outlook as a child who'd been in care was already pretty bleak. There were more than enough stats to bear that out.

And our job in this process was apparently clear. It seemed that rather than our usual job – of loving and nurturing her with a view to her staying in a family setting – ours, even – we were essentially just being asked to keep things calm and contain her. To keep her out of trouble for as long as possible, until she had a 'release date', as if our home was just a half-way house for rehabilitating prisoners.

I didn't need to think hard to know there were two ways this could go. It could either be extremely easy, or the complete opposite – and how it played out would be largely up to Mike and me. We could take Danny at his word – feed Keeley, clothe her, provide bed and board and a reasonable amount of boundaries for her – and, all the while, without paying too close attention to whatever else her life consisted of, including her charming little phone-sex business. After all, that was all we were being asked to do.

Or, to use Mike's words, I could instead 'do a Casey' – try my level best to help change her mind about rejecting the system, and the attendant depressing outlook that might lead to. To do what I could to stop her becoming another component that made up those same statistics – the ones that proved a childhood in the care system meant a life of, at best, chronic under-achievement, unemployment (without GCSEs she had little to offer an employer) and, at worst, a life of criminality, drugs or worse; one destined to follow the path set by her mother, and so ensuring that the cycle continued.

A path which could so easily start from a bedroom in some grotty flat and a mobile phone. With no Casey snooping outside to curtail her paying hobby, what was to stop her, after all? As she unpacked her possessions upstairs, oblivious, I made my choice. Whether she liked it or not (and if Danny was right, she definitely wouldn't like it) I decided I was going to do a Casey.

Keeley didn't need calling down in the end. She appeared in the dining room half an hour or so into the meeting, red in the face from her unpacking exertions, and, having first visited the kitchen, holding a glass of water. I pulled out the chair between Danny and me. 'We've pretty much done all the boring stuff now,' he told her. 'Just need to hear your thoughts now, about staying here – if you have any? Is there anything you need to ask me while I'm here, Keels?'

Keeley glanced around the table. 'So I am going to be staying here, then, am I? I mean, that's fine by me,' she said, gracing me with a smile. 'Anywhere so long as I don't have to go back *there*. And it's only till I'm sixteen, anyways, so it's all good,' she finished.

I resisted the urge to pitch in with 'you're welcome', and catching my eye – and perhaps my thought process – Danny grinned.

'Don't worry, we hear you loud and clear, Keels,' he said. 'And yes, Casey has *very* kindly agreed that you can stay here for a while. But like anywhere,' he went on, leaning forward for emphasis, 'the Watsons have rules, and I expect you to heed them, okay? If you're expecting me to go out on a limb and sort you out some accommodation for after your birthday, then you have to do your bit, too, okay? Following the rules, as I've told you before, is a normal part of life. We all have to do it and you're no exception.'

It was obviously a conversation they'd had several times before. 'Yeah, yeah, I know,' Keeley replied, nodding, 'I get it. I have to behave myself. And I have been.'

Danny's gaze became stern, which put years on him. Which was good. 'Well, from what I hear,' he went on, 'you don't quite "get it", Keeley. Last time I checked, having phone sex, or whatever it is you call it, *isn't* playing by the rule book. And you know that.' His face grew sterner still and Keeley shrank a little in her seat, pulling a face like a resentful ten-year-old. 'Keeley, how can I tell anyone – let alone put it down on paper, in all conscience – that you are shaping up to being a responsible adult when you do things like this? What were you *thinking*?'

The resentful ten-year-old changed into an angry teen-ager again. '*God*,' Keeley snapped, clearly reverting to knee-jerk hostility now she'd been skewered. 'I've already had a bollocking for that, haven't I? *And* I've got the coppers coming round to have a go at me. Can't you just *leave* it now?' she finished.

Danny shook his head. 'No, I can't. Not until I'm quite sure you understand how not on all that sort of thing is. It's simply not something a fifteen-year-old should be doing. You could be speaking to anyone, and you know it.'

Keeley huffed, crossed her arms across her chest, then changed her mind, and held her hands up in appeasement. 'Okay,' she said, 'Okay. I *get* it. Naughty Keeley. My bad. I won't do it again. I swear down. Now, can I go finish my room?'

'You promise me?' Danny said. 'A lot depends on this, Keeley.'

'*Honestly*. I *promise* you,' she said, smiling once again sweetly.

She got up again, then, her part in proceedings apparently over, and managed to leave us without too much of a flounce.

Danny glanced at John and me in turn as he sorted out the various forms we'd need to sign. 'Hmm. I wouldn't bank on it,' he said.

Chapter 7

'I won't do it again.' 'I'm almost sixteen.' 'You don't need to flap.' Over and over.

For the next couple of weeks, as Keeley began to settle in, it was as if those three statements were on a continuous repeating loop. And if I was certain of anything – I was still feeling my way with her, after all – it was that only one of those statements was true.

I'd been fairly certain about the first one the very same day that I'd been introduced to Danny. And not just because of his weary-sounding warning, key though that was, because he obviously knew his young charge well. No, it became more obvious once he'd left and, the prom-ised half-hour later, the policemen had turned up to deliver Keeley her lecture.

I had initially been optimistic that their visit would not be in vain. One in uniform, and both old enough to look appropriately paternal, one was a standard community support officer, the other the oddly named 'safer care' officer John had mentioned, whose job it apparently was

65

to raise consciousness among teens about the growing problem of online grooming and abuse.

'We go into schools, too,' he was explaining, once I'd shown them into the living room. 'Kind of dial a doom merchant, if you like. But if these kids had even half an idea of the sort of things we're seeing ...' He trailed off then, shaking his head.

Keeley had come back down to meet them with a polite enough smile, but it didn't quite manage to camouflage (at least for me) the resigned air of someone all too aware that what they had to do was simply go through the motions. She was used to all this, and she played it like a pro, particularly when they showed her a film of a girl being groomed (they'd brought their own laptop for the purpose), opening her greeny-brown eyes ever wider, acting the proverbial shocked innocent, and generally giving the impression that she was woefully impressionable herself.

She even – dare I say it – seemed to enjoy it. Well, if 'enjoying' it is strictly the right word. And, perhaps surprisingly, I did too. Though, like the police officers, I'd been doing my job long enough to know more than I wanted to about such matters, it was fascinating to see it spelled out so clearly how the process took place – not least the amount of time and effort these evil characters put into it.

The film was made in documentary style, featuring a young girl of thirteen, played by an actress. It spelled out the various grooming stages. The girl believed for weeks that she was chatting to a boy of around her own age who lived locally – and why wouldn't she? His Facebook page looked entirely genuine. They chatted online for several weeks, the relationship slowly developing, and, again, nothing about what the girl (or indeed I) was seeing from his posts and messages would ring alarm bells in any way.

And, as often happens within the other-worldly world of online conversations, as their relationship became closer, so did their conversations, and, driven by the usual hormones, became increasingly sexual too.

And as night apparently follows day in our new permissive, sexualised, highly connected world, she agreed to send him some video clips – of the sort of thing Keeley had been describing on the phone.

The very next day, she was then mortified to discover that the images and clips had been shared right across social media.

'And not just *her* social media,' the officer pointed out grimly. 'This was no innocent boy. Those videos would have been shared by all sorts, you get me?'

Keeley nodded meekly, and then again, as the narrator went on to explain that this was based on a real case, and that the girl had been so traumatised that she'd become clinically depressed, and was unable to return to school; in the end the family had decided they had no choice but to up sticks and relocate to a different part of the country.

All very serious, but I could tick off the ways in which it wouldn't be of much help. Keeley had no family to become traumatised for her. Keeley didn't care a jot about school. Keeley was savvy. Keeley was street-smart and blooded. Keeley was nothing like this girl.

Still, she accepted the leaflet the officers gave her, and I knew they left feeling they'd achieved something good. And perhaps they had. Perhaps something useful had sunk in. Perhaps Keeley wasn't quite as hardened as she claimed to be.

But once they'd gone any hope of that was dispatched in short order.

'That's the thing,' she mused, flicking through the leaflet as I washed up the officers' mugs.

'What's the thing?' I asked.

'I mean, it's all very helpful and that,' she said. 'You know, educating girls about this sort of stuff. But, like, do they really think I'm that naïve? That's the point. I'm not stupid. *I'm* in control, aren't I? Because I already *know* the sort of men I'm dealing with, don't I?'

I gaped.

'Sorry, *did*,' she corrected quickly. 'Cross my heart, Casey.' She did so. 'I won't do it again.'

And it seemed, over the ensuing days, that she was at least being as good as her word. Well, as far as I could tell, and I was checking on her often. If I was going to commit to doing what I could for her, a few minor intrusions on her privacy were, as far as I was concerned, a justifiable means to an end.

But it soon became clear that what went on inside the house was the least of our worries. Actually *keeping* her in it was much more of a concern.

I knew Danny had spelled out that the education door was pretty much locked now, but I came back to it again and again. Not with Keeley herself – she'd made it amply clear there was no conversation to be had there – but in my head, because not going to school was one thing, but not doing anything at all was insane, especially for a bright girl like her.

One of my mum's favourite sayings when I was growing up was that the devil finds work for idle hands to do. And she was right, of course, as life had shown me again and again. A human without purpose isn't generally in the best place, but a child without purpose is a whole other animal – too much time on their hands and it's so often the case that they get into all kinds of mischief.

Not that I knew what sort of things Keeley got up to. Only that she was out of the house, day and evening, from the very next day on – as if the weekend (the upheavals, the lectures and meetings) had merely been an interruption in her busy schedule.

A schedule that, amazingly, appeared to be carrying on regardless despite her being some twenty-five miles from her usual stomping ground, far away on the other side of town. I wondered again at the foster home she'd come from, and the freedoms she seemed to take so much for granted. Had she been given no boundaries at all?

'I'm a naturally friendly person,' was Keeley's answer the first time I asked her where she was off to, and with whom. 'I like to get out and about and meet new people and stuff. My old mates come over as well. They get the train,' she added helpfully. 'So I meet them in town and we just hang about.'

'They're not in school either?' I asked. It seemed a reasonable enough question. Either they didn't attend, like her, which wasn't the best scenario ever, or they were a good bit older, which wasn't very edifying either – not when coupled with the words 'hanging about'.

Though least edifying was the whole 'hanging about in town' scenario, period. 'Doing what?' I asked. 'What do you find to do exactly?'

She gave me what my mum would have called an old-fashioned look. 'We don't sit around doing drugs, Casey, if that's what you're thinking. Anyway, I'm almost sixteen, so you really don't need to flap about it.'

So that was me told. As if being 'nearly sixteen' was akin to being 'nearly twenty-five'. Which it wasn't, so it didn't stop me flapping in the slightest. For what it was worth, I believed her on the 'not doing drugs' front – she seemed altogether too self-possessed. And, as sometimes happened (praise be) with the children of addicts, perhaps she was still haunted by the loss of her mother to heroin, and avoided all drugs as a consequence.

But there was no getting away from the fact that she would be offered drugs, because they were everywhere. No way was I going to be naïve about the likelihood that some of her friends *did* do drugs, and might also be involved in petty crime. How long before her assurances would begin to ring hollow? When a truanting kid who was just 'hanging out' became another drop-out, another chronic social ill.

No, if I wanted to help Keeley, I needed to try and get her off the streets, and despite Danny's apparent resistance to the idea, by mid-week, with her out, and Tyler in school, I was in full-on bothersome mode, bothering John, bothering ELAC (Education for Looked After Children) for more information on her school history, and most of all bothering Danny himself – to get them to revisit the idea that, even if she wasn't going back to school, she should be persuaded of the merits of doing *something*.

'The problem,' Danny said, having returned my most recent call, 'is that we are pretty much out of options. Keeley's done with school, as you know, and we've been here before. Twice now, I've got her back into mainstream education, and both times she really put her heart and soul into it – as in making sure she got excluded without delay.'

'I do get that,' I said. 'And I have read the file, so I'm not suggesting I try and get her enrolled in Tyler's or anything. But it doesn't have to be a school, does it? Not a mainstream one, anyway. Ours has a thing called a "Reach for Success" programme – John might have mentioned it? I used to work there and I helped set it up. She could attend there – I've already checked with them – even if only part time.'

I could hear Danny's sigh. 'We've been there as well. She's been to various alternative learning units during the time I've been with her – you'll see it all when you get her personal education plan – some with the luxury of just four or five pupils. And she *still* doesn't cooperate. Threats of permanent exclusion are exactly what she wants. And the more that's happened the less anyone else has wanted to take her. You know how it goes.'

I came back again to this foster family who had apparently decided that Keeley's lack of education was no biggie.

How did that work? Had they just run out of energy to argue the point with her? Had they too been sold the whole 'I'm offskies' line? Even if they hadn't before, I thought darkly, they most definitely had now. Was that what she'd been hoping for all along?

And what about her little sister? Was she in school? I imagined so. 'But, Danny, don't the council have a duty to ensure she's educated?' I persisted. I'd been out of the world of school for a while, and it hadn't come up in my fostering, but I couldn't believe that wasn't so.

But it apparently wasn't. 'They have a duty to offer her college-style or employment training,' Danny said. 'But if she chooses not to do it – if she's determined to go off and find herself a job – then, in practice, there is little they can do at this stage. Not given her age. Were her birthday later in the school year it might be different. Or if she was sitting exams, of course. But would it really? In practice? I'm not sure. No, her old school have pretty much washed their hands of her now, and she's resistant to any suggestions about college. She just wants to get to sixteen, get herself a flat and a job.'

'Another job, you mean,' I said. 'She's already got one.'

'Oh, God. She's not still at that in the house, is she?'

'I have no idea, Danny – how would I? She could be at it half the night. And what she gets up to when she's *not* at home I have absolutely no idea.'

Another sigh. 'It's not the best situation, is it?' he conceded.

'You're telling me,' I said. 'What about the sister, Jade? Maybe she could have some influence? Keeley tells me they're close. How are things with her? I assume she's going to school okay.'

'As far as I know, yes. She's in mainstream education and doing really well by all accounts. As was Keeley at one time. I promise you. I've gone back and read everything on her file. As you'll be able to do yourself when you get it all in the post.'

'That's a good point,' I pointed out. 'When's it all coming anyway? I could really do with a fuller picture of her background.'

'Okay, I'll chase it,' he said, as if I'd been nagging him for days. He sounded defensive and I realised I wasn't sure what he was even promising. That Keeley had been doing well? Or that he'd done his research? Perhaps he too was weary of trying to influence Keeley. *Till she wasn't doing well*, I mused to myself. 'Thank you,' I said out loud. 'I appreciate it.'

'Seriously,' he said, back in his groove, 'we have tried. And over quite a long period. She started going downhill around the start of year nine. Foster parents in and out. Detentions. The usual thing. Just a downward trajectory. Increasing non-attendance. Lack of motivation. She wasn't in a good place, was she? Perhaps it had all begun to really hit home for her. You know how it sometimes goes.'

But didn't *need* to go, surely? It took a lot of effort from all parties to produce such a dispiriting *fait accompli*. It seemed criminal that a bright kid like Keeley should be languishing outside education, and even more so that the school seemed to have turned a blind eye for so long. But the trouble was that I could completely understand it. I had *seen* it. So I knew all too well how hard it was to engage an older child who fought tooth and nail against the system. Even if Keeley hadn't been especially disruptive, just having a child in class who truanted regularly and had fallen way behind everyone else could impact seriously on all the others – the ones who did want to do well – taking up a massive chunk of their teachers' time and attention just by virtue of being there. No, it was no wonder that teachers sometimes took the view that losing one for the greater good was the better way. Not so much a blind eye as a conscious decision.

'So what's been going on? You know, since then. Has she had any schooling at all?'

'Not much,' Danny said. 'By the time I took the case on they'd done all the usual. She'd had mentoring, detentions, been excluded and so on. She'd also had a spell at a different school. ELAC had organised home schooling for her, and that was ongoing for a bit. Then back in school. Then not, and now she's in year 11 … well, hypothetically …

'Look,' he said. 'The last thing I want is to put you off trying – not least because it's bound to be challenging having her around the house all the time. You know where we are with her – she doesn't want to continue with her education, period. But if you can persuade her otherwise – find her some vocational college course or something that she feels enthusiastic about – that would be great. Perhaps this whole upheaval will turn out to have been a good thing; shaken everyone out of just accepting the status quo. Shaken her out of her rut, even. And I'm sure

ELAC could swing something, even if it's mid-term and temporary, so if you want to get a prospectus, be my guest. Or I could do it if you like? Save you having to?'

I wasn't directing it at Danny, because I didn't have all the facts, but it seemed to me that these were options that should have been discussed yonks ago, shouldn't they? And I just couldn't get my head round the mentality of her last foster carers. Why had they *allowed* things to get this bad? *Had* they just given up on her?

I told Danny I'd sort out a college prospectus myself and, after ringing off and ordering a print one from their website, I called John, to update him, and to put the question to him too.

'Who knows,' he said. 'And I doubt we will find out any time soon either. But I've read more of Keeley's file now' – so he, too, had more flipping information than I had – 'and my hunch is that when they realised they'd taken on more than they could deal with they started to regret taking her on. Maybe she hit puberty and started acting out – perhaps her past – not to mention her future – was finally catching up with her, and they didn't know how to manage her. Maybe they reckoned she was a bad influence on the younger one. Jade, isn't it?'

'Who she tells me she's very close to,' I said. 'And I believe her.'

'Which makes her actions over last weekend rather precipitous, don't you think? At least, if we all believe they're going to be unsubstantiated, that is. Which seems likely. All a bit of a puzzle, isn't it? Either way, you know what I think? I think they're probably fine with it. Perhaps they were relieved – they've certainly not been in uproar about it, by all accounts. Which makes me even surer it's all fluff. That it's a game they know she's playing. A game they are happy to go along with because it's turned out to be a gift – they know it has no substance, but at the same time it means they can wash their hands of her, without recriminations.'

That term again. Was that her lot in life? To be a child who everyone wanted to wash their hands of?

Things must have been bad at the Burkes, then, I decided. They must have been if it was preferable to be accused of making sexual advances than to continue to foster the poor girl. And that was another thing. There didn't seem to be any progress on that front; something I'd have thought would have been nothing short of critical – because if it turned out that Mr Burke *had* done something untoward, then surely their adopted daughter Jade would also be classed as being at risk. Yet there was nothing. Not a peep. And no one seemed anxious to push things. Every time I asked it was simply 'ongoing'.

As was Keeley's loose attachment to the Watson family rules.

Despite her assurances to Danny that she knew toeing the line at ours was the key to her promised freedom, by the Sunday evening of the second week I was feeling more than a little frazzled by her smiling disregard for boundaries.

I knew what we'd taken on, of course, because it had already been made clear: a girl old enough to enjoy a measure of freedom – her phone and her social life, not to mention her self-destructive choices about schooling. But it was hard to square that with our other responsibility – to Tyler, our son, who was older than she was, and enjoyed no such parental latitude.

And Keeley seemed to enjoy wielding her power. If we told her to be in by nine, it would be half past, and if we said half past, then it would be ten. And so on it went, with Mike and me trying to rein her in, by insisting that the consequences of returning home late one night would be that she had to be in the following evening an hour earlier. But we were wasting our breath. Whatever we said, she came in when it suited her. Never so long after the agreed time that we'd have to send out a search party, but just late enough to deliver a clear message – that, despite the tossed out 'sorry I'm late' apologies and ridiculous excuses she always offered, she would come home when it suited *her*.

It was Tyler I felt for, particularly. He knew all too well that if he slipped out of line there would be consequences. For a start I would have taken his phone away from him for a period, and restricted his time on the internet.

With Keeley it wasn't as simple. Her phone was her own and I had no right to take it from her, which meant that she could access the internet any time she wanted to; one of the biggest modern headaches for foster carers. And what was true for her school was true for us too. Our only recourse, when it came to Keeley flouting our family rules, was to tell John we didn't want to hang on to her after all. That we'd wash our hands of her as well.

Did she want that? Did she care if she was once again moved on? With mere weeks to go till she could move on in life alone, I suspected her only reason for keeping us sweet was to ensure she kept Danny sweet and so got what she was really after – supported lodgings and a chance to run her life herself.

'Perhaps we should call her bluff and start delivering ultimatums,' Mike suggested. But I couldn't yet agree. That would play right into her hands – her taste for getting expelled made that obvious – and I wasn't ready to do that. No, I'd stick with it and do my best to try and interest her in some kind of college course, even if only a couple of days a week and even if it involved an element of manipulation, such as making her signed-off pathway plan conditional upon it. Because I was sure that if she had something positive to focus on she'd be less inclined to wander the streets.

Right now, though, she breezed into the house as cool as you like, making only the most cursory nod towards an apology as she swept in.

'Before you start ...' she said, 'my phone died and I had no idea what time it was. By the time I saw anyone to ask, I was already fifteen minutes late, so I had to literally run all the way home.'

If she was expecting a round of applause for her efforts she was about to be disappointed. Mike glared at her and I could tell he was angrier than she probably realised, having been interrupted in the middle of helping Tyler with some revision for an upcoming test. And as she banged the side door shut, she then added to his irritation, having caused enough air turbulence to send several sheets of A4 wafting off the kitchen table.

'Yeah, right, great job, well done,' said Tyler.

Mike stood up and I sensed an impending flash point. 'That's no excuse, Keeley,' he said, his voice low and stern as he towered over her. 'And did you think we came down in the last shower of rain? Eh? Don't you think we've heard every excuse in the book?' He raised a hand. Pointed a finger. '*Every* time, Keeley. Every single time, we've given you another chance. And every time you promise you'll do better. Well, young lady,' he said, and I could see just how angry he was, 'now I'm making *you* a promise. The very next time you're so much as five minutes late you will be grounded the following night. Do it again, and you'll be grounded for *two* nights. We're not having it. It ends right this minute. Do you understand?'

I think Keeley must have been a little shocked to hear Mike speak so harshly. I was too, to be truthful, because it wasn't often that he lost his temper, especially with one of the foster kids. But I couldn't blame him. I knew he was more annoyed that Tyler was witness to all of it and I knew what he was thinking about that too. He needed to be cross. To assert his authority. If not, how long before Tyler, quite reasonably, began to question how much she was getting away with?

I watched Keeley's expression run through various options. And perhaps – sensibly – opt for contrition.

'I am sorry, Mike, *honest*,' she said, sounding sincere. 'And look, my phone *is* dead.' She held it up as evidence. He ignored it, instead reaching down to gather up the papers.

'C'mon, son,' he said to Tyler. 'Let's finish this off in the dining room.' The coldest of cold shoulders.

Keeley shrugged, though half-heartedly. Mike wasn't even looking. And as they left the kitchen she slipped her phone back into her pocket. Which was interesting. I'd have expected her to fall desperately upon her charger. It was her lifeline to everything that mattered to her, after all.

But maybe not right now this minute.

'I've saved you a Sunday dinner,' I said, trying my best to sound impartial. I really didn't want it to look like Mike and I were playing good cop, bad cop. Some rules were sacrosanct – and the two of us presenting a united parental front was one of them. I knew that was the best way, from long experience. But neither did I want Keeley to feel that the whole world and its uncle were against her. Cool was sufficient. Not ice-cold. 'You hungry?' I added.

She nodded. Then she sat down and, with no phone to stare at, stared across the hall to where Mike and Tyler now were instead. An outsider looking in? I sort of hoped so. Another feature of parenting was working with the knowledge that all children, whatever their age or their background, craved the approval of those adults they respected. Early days, yes, but I wondered if this was true of Keeley and Mike.

Perhaps so. I was just programming the microwave when she spoke. 'Bit harsh,' she observed. 'I *was* telling the truth, honest. He didn't need to go off on one like that. All shouty.'

I watched the plate turn behind the glass and considered how to respond. 'What did you expect, love?' I said mildly. 'You've been pushing it and pushing it. You've been late almost every single night you've been out. It's worrying for us.'

'I told you, I'm *fine*.'

'*You* knowing you're fine is irrelevant, Keeley. Even *us* believing you're fine is irrelevant, for that matter. We have a job to do. A responsibility for you, whether you like it or not. Don't you understand that? That's why Mike's annoyed with you. Because this is all so exhausting and we really don't need it. Surely you can see that?'

The microwave pinged and I grabbed a cloth to pull the plate out. 'Here,' I said. 'Get on the outside of that and let's hear no more about it. And tomorrow –'

'Oh, I meant to say. Danny's coming round. And his manager, I think. Possibly.' She speared a potato.

'Oh, really? I didn't know anything about that.'

'You won't have. Well, you might have. But you will do.'

'I'm losing track, love.'

'That's why my phone died. 'Cos I was on the phone to him for so long. He's gone off on one too.' She glanced pointedly across to the other room.

'Why? What about?'

'Because I told him I made it up.'

There was a moment of incomprehension before the penny dropped. 'What, about your foster father?'

'Of course about him,' she said, putting the potato in her mouth. 'Who else?'

I pulled a chair out and sat down. 'You really mean that? That he never touched you? That you did make it all up?'

'Course I did,' she said, seeming completely unconcerned. 'I hate him. I told you. And I had to say something, didn't I? I'd tried everything else to get them to move me – Danny knows that – and they wouldn't. But saying that meant they had to. Anyway, it's done now. So I don't know what he's flapping about. It's all good.'

It's not often that I'm speechless, but I came pretty close. I just couldn't get my head round the calm way she was telling me. If I'd been concerned that she'd falsely made such a serious allegation in the first place, the insouciant way she was admitting that she'd made it all up was on a whole other level. She'd put an entire family through the trauma of what surely must have followed, yet it was like water off a duck's back. It beggared belief.

'No it's not "all good", Keeley,' I eventually said. 'It's not good at all. You could have ruined their bloody lives!'

Again a shrug. 'They're too dumb. Honest, it won't have even bothered them. And it had to be something bad or they'd have been under pressure to have me back again, wouldn't they? Which they didn't want. *Really*,' she added, presumably seeing my expression. 'You don't know what they're like. You don't know what *he's* like.' She moved on to a stuffing ball. 'Honest, it's win-win, if you ask me.'

Which struck me as the saddest interpretation of the word 'win' I'd ever heard. I really didn't know this girl at all.

Chapter 8

'Well, it's only what we all suspected, isn't it?' said Mike. 'Poor couple. What a horrendous thing to be put through.'

It had ended up being a long night. The display on the bedside clock glowed its inevitable message to prove it. That there were far too few hours of the night left. We should really stop discussing this and go to sleep.

'And it could have been us,' I said. '*You*. That's what I keep coming back to. It was so calculated. She wanted out and she knew how to get out. God, how damaged and cynical must she be? Talk about biting the hand that feeds you.'

'I wonder what his real crime was?' Mike mused. 'We know almost nothing about either of them, after all. Though the fact that they didn't class the other girl as "at risk" tells us lots. Had they so much as a whisper of a doubt they would have acted right away and removed her. And they're foster carers, for God's sake. They'd have been scrutinised minutely. *And* they adopted. So ditto. You know, Case, I'm beginning to feel distinctly less enthusiastic about us keeping this girl.'

I understood. I felt likewise. I didn't want to, but I did. Much as I kept trying to tell myself that it was the behaviour, not the child – that Keeley was a victim, and that the traumas of her childhood were at the root of how she was now – I felt the same sense of gloom as my husband did about her future. I stared up at the ceiling, contemplating defeat. Perhaps it was too late to help her. Everyone else seemed to think so. She was almost sixteen now, as she kept on reminding us. Perhaps I was being way too idealistic to believe we could help turn things around for her. Why should we succeed where everyone else had failed?

'I know …' I began.

'You know what I think?' Mike said. 'I think this crisis has been a long time in the making. The poor bloke's probably been way too soft with her, for years. And the more she's got away with, the more powerful she's become. You know what they say about creating a monster. Well, perhaps by being too soft he's created one in her. He probably started out like we did, don't you think? Making allowances. Overlooking the coming home late. The back chat. The swearing. The attitude. Then, before he knew it, Keeley was in control. Till he snapped. Laid the law down. And, bingo, she's kicked back by doing this. She's simply playing the system. It's textbook.'

'I can't allow myself to believe she could be that manipulative or heartless,' I said, even though a part of me so easily could. Teenagers – your own teenagers – could run rings round you. Everyone knew that. So teenagers who had no love or respect for you to temper their excesses –

well, as Mike said, this sort of thing happened all the time, particularly with kids who'd become so damaged that they had no attachments to care about. They had nothing to lose.

'I can,' Mike said.

'Yes, but perhaps it was just a moment of madness. We have to give her the benefit of the doubt about that. A spur of the moment thing, said on impulse, that snowballed out of control. We hardly know her, do we? This whole thing with Danny. Her texting him out of the blue like that. She might not have said as much, but perhaps she's been looking for an opportunity to set things straight since day one.'

I was saying it as much to convince myself as Mike. And he didn't seem convinced at all. In fact, he snorted. 'Maybe so, Casey, but I tell you what – she's not going to be playing us for fools, that's for sure. And I hope there's going to be some retribution from social services about it. Look at the trouble she's caused.' He reached across to switch off his bedside light. 'Love, I'm not sure we shouldn't just call John and ask him to find somewhere else for her. I'm not sure we want her here, around Tyler. Are you?'

'I don't know,' I said. 'Let's sleep on it, eh? Everything always seems better in the morning.'

But would it? *Should* we wash our hands of her too?

Danny called me only seconds after Tyler left for school the following morning.

'It's not too early, is it?' he asked. 'Only I have some news to share.'

'If it's what I'm thinking it is, then Keeley's already told me.'

'Oh, she has, has she? What did she say?'

'Very little really. Just trotted it out as if it was nothing. As if it were a perfectly reasonable thing to do. And said you were coming over today?'

'No, I won't be. I don't think there's any need. Unless you want me to, that is. I'll be busy enough letting everyone know what the score is. I'm going to go round to see the Burkes as soon as I've finished making my calls. I'm sure they will be mightily relieved, aren't you?'

'Keeley didn't seem to think they'd be worried in the first place. She seems to think she's done them a favour by doing what she did. Which I really can't get my head round. They must feel so manipulated.'

'Well, they have been,' Danny said, 'but I'm also relieved. We were on very thin ice conducting an investigation like that without removing their adopted daughter from them, as you probably know. Still, at least we can move on now. And hopefully Keeley can too.'

'So that's the end of it? Is no one going to speak to Keeley? You know, officially? Make her aware of the seriousness of what she's done?'

'I don't know yet. I'll need to speak to my manager. But, to be honest, I'm not sure what purpose it would serve now. And I'm sure you'll have already made that clear to her. Speaking of which, how have things been since we last spoke?'

'Trying,' I said. 'She still seems determined to test us. Going out God knows where. Coming in when she feels like it. Staying up late, sleeping in late. Doing pretty much what she pleases. Which amounts to very little as far as I can see.'

'But you're still aiming to try and get her onto a college course?'

He spoke as if he didn't hold out much hope. And perhaps I shouldn't either. And I wavered for a moment, wondering if I should share my feelings with him. Let him know that Mike and I had reached a decision. That, as of today, Keeley was living with us on borrowed time. That we were going to give it a week and if she didn't shape up and give us something positive to work on, I'd be having a rather different conversation with him in seven days' time.

But there was no point in adding yet another negative to the pile. 'My absolute level best,' I assured him.

I left Keeley to sleep till I'd done all my chores, and, determined to maintain my positive mindset, decided that the matter was closed. So when she came down, bleary-eyed (had her night been sleepless too?), I simply told her that Danny wouldn't be coming round to deliver any lectures, and that as far as I was concerned we'd draw a line under it all.

'Good,' she said. 'And they can all move on with their sad little lives now, can't they? And Jade'll be okay. That's the main thing.'

Once again, I was struck by how flippant her tone was. But elected to ignore it. She'd probably spent years perfecting it, after all. 'Yes, she will,' I said. 'But you're the one I'm interested in currently. D'you want some break-fast? Bacon sandwich? I'm going to have one. Then we're going to sit down and talk about what we're going to do with you.'

'*Do* with me?'

'Do with you. As in finding something for you *to* do. As in something more constructive than just hanging about.'

'What, you mean work?'

'No, I mean your *education*. I know you're allergic to the word school, but –'

'Because it's *pointless*. I *hate* it. And I'm rubbish at it, too. Just ask them. They all think I'm thick, and I am.'

I pulled strips of bacon apart and put them into the pan. 'You absolutely are *not*,' I said firmly.

'How would you know?' she said, yanking the cutlery drawer open. 'You're not one of my teachers.'

Her voice was only mildly combative; more as if she was trotting out a well-worn line. 'I don't need to be,' I said. 'I have eyes and ears, don't I? And I can think of lots of things that you're good at.'

'Like what?'

'You're very organised,' I said, realising I'd now put myself in a situation where I had to think on the hoof. She'd have a keen nose for being patronised, I was sure. 'You've only to look at your room to see that. To get that much stuff shoehorned into a bedroom is a remarkable skill to have, believe me. And – dare I say it – you are also resourceful. Just look at how you manipulated everything so that you could move house, for instance – even if you did it in a manner that I sincerely hope you won't be trying

88

again. And you're well spoken,' I hurried on. Maybe best we gloss over all that. 'Well, most of the time, anyway. You're polite. You're intelligent. How could anyone possibly think you're "thick", as you put it? It strikes me that the only one who thinks that is you.'

I turned over the bacon while she pulled out two plates from the cupboard. 'And – see? – you don't need to be told to do things all the time. You have initiative, and you use it, and that's a real sign of intelligence. To be honest, Keeley, I'm not even sure you even think you *are* thick. I think you just don't like anyone telling you what to do. And you like to make it easy for yourself to duck out of things you don't think have value. Like going to school. I think you peddle this line about being useless because you choose to. Brown or white?'

It was a long speech – definitely longer than I'd intended. And I'd clearly touched a nerve. Or struck a chord, or something. Because as I dished up the bacon on the bread she'd already buttered she seemed deep in thought.

'Penny for them,' I said, as she squirted on ketchup.

'What?'

'For your thoughts. What's going on in there currently?'

'It's their fault. They ruined everything. You do know that, don't you?'

'Who did? Your foster parents?'

'No, the *social*. When they took me away.'

She stopped to take a bite, and I did too. She was on a train of thought and I didn't want to accidentally derail it. She seemed in the mood to state her case.

'It was fine before they stuck their nose in. I was going to school. I *liked* school.'

'You were still in primary school then, yes?'

She nodded. 'They had no idea. They just decided stuff that they didn't know anything about.' Her tone was getting a little more strident now. 'I did everything. They didn't realise. They thought I was just some shitty kid, but I did everything.' I let the word lie. 'I had to. I *wanted* to. You know, to help Mum out, because she was sick all the time. I did. I did everything.' She put the sandwich down to count on her fingers. 'I did the cooking. Did the washing. Paid the milkman. Put the bins out. I even took Harvey to the doctors when he had chickenpox. Did you know that? I bet they didn't put *that* on my file.'

Her eyes glittered. Her voice challenged me. This was already the longest and most meaningful conversation we'd had since she'd come to us. I shook my head. 'No, I didn't. But I'm not sure I know any ten-year-olds who'd have the presence of mind to do that.' I picked up my coffee. 'You should be very proud of yourself, Keeley. What are the rest of their names? Your brothers and sisters? Harvey is the youngest, right?' She nodded. 'And the others? We've not chatted about them yet, have we? Two of each, is that right?'

'Aaron and Harvey are the boys. Harvey's the baby. Aaron was six when they took me away.' She frowned. 'My sisters are Courtney – she was four. And then Lily. She was two.'

'And you took care of all of them.'

She looked surprised that I even asked. 'Course I did. I told you. I mean Mum did too. They don't realise. They made out like she was *so* useless. But she wasn't all the time. She didn't want to be. It wasn't like she didn't *try*. She tried her *best*,' she added plaintively.

I wondered about the conversations the ten-year-old Keeley had with whoever had become responsible for making the horrible decision to dismantle every foundation she'd ever known. A horrible, horrible job.

I also wondered if there was any mileage in speaking to someone about her past a bit more, before pressing on with her future. Was there any point? Were those ties completely severed now? Presumably someone knew the whereabouts of her siblings. It wasn't the time to ask Keeley about that, however, not least because it could – probably would – be a road to nowhere. Or else surely it would have been looked into before.

I needed the full picture. But without the paperwork Danny had promised, I still didn't have it. So instead I just nodded in agreement. 'I'm sure she did, Keeley.' I said. What mother wouldn't, after all? Well, in theory. I knew nothing about Keeley's mum, did I? Perhaps she was an entirely feckless mother, with heroin her only true love.

But listening to the way Keeley spoke, I suspected there must have been moments of light in the darkness. Love. At least flowing in that direction. Or perhaps she had just reprocessed her memories to make them easier to live with. Created a fantasy that was easier to bear than the reality. Of a loving mother, of giggling, clean, fresh-faced siblings. Of a functional, happy household. Almost none of this could be true. That much was obvious. And lovely as Keeley's version of her past might be, I knew she wouldn't be able to properly move on until she was emotionally strong enough to deal with the real past. To accept that it wasn't all rainbows and fluff.

Right now, though, she was clearly in absolutely no doubt where the real villainy lay.

'She *did*,' she said. 'She couldn't help being ill, could she?

That word 'ill' again. My heart went out to her. How else was she going to process her mother's addiction? Except by wrapping it up in pretty paper and tying it with a ribbon? And wasn't addiction a type of illness anyway?

But this wasn't the moment to ignite a wave of fury at those whom she saw as having ruined everything. Not yet. 'And having that responsibility has clearly been good for you,' I said briskly. 'However bad everything else must seem. You're a proper can-do person, Keeley, and you need to find something you *want* to do. Not write yourself off before you're even an adult. Come on, think. What *do* you like doing?' I nodded towards the living room. 'I have a prospectus for you to look at, bristling with courses you could have a stab at. How about catering? You said you always used to do the cooking, didn't you? Or child care, maybe? Or hairdressing? Hair and beauty, maybe? What am I even saying?' I added, grinning. 'You would be *perfect* for hair and beauty. What do you say? Can I tempt you to take a look?'

Keeley picked up my empty plate and stacked it on top of her own. 'Did I tell you?' she said, as she pushed her chair back to rise. 'My mum was a hairdresser when she left school. You know, before having us and everything.'

Progress, I thought, mentally crossing my fingers. At last.

And then, almost as if to physically underline it, I heard the letter box squeak and the sound of a heavy envelope landing on the mat. Keeley's notes, finally. Which would be my bedtime reading that night. What a difference a couple of hours could make.

Chapter 9

To my acute disappointment, not to mention sadness, Keeley's notes didn't make for the best reading. There was little in them that I didn't already know, and what little I hadn't known only served to confirm that there *had* been a reason for her being parted from her siblings, in the form of a big question mark hanging over her. A question mark about her that had effectively sealed her fate. And all sparked by a disclosure from a four-year-old.

It was usual, at the point when children are removed into care following a crisis, for any who are old enough to be interviewed. In the case of the McAlister children, this duly happened, the four- and six-year-olds, Courtney and Aaron (who'd been billeted together), both having been questioned about what happened on the night when the police came.

Mike's assumption had been right. The children had initially been fostered separately for practical reasons, there being no one available to take them all. So it was that Keeley was fostered on her own, the middle two to a temporary foster home together, and the babies – the ones with the best chance of an untroubled future – into foster care alone, with a view to being quickly adopted. All of which I already knew, of course.

What I hadn't known, however, was that, at that point, there'd been no plan to separate them permanently. Even with the younger two going up for adoption that didn't preclude some sort of contact being maintained. And perhaps they'd have been reunited – at least in terms of regular contact – but for one thing. That the four-year-old, Courtney, when questioned about the man who'd done horrible things to her, had mentioned that Keeley had not only been there, but had also been the one 'guarding the door'. She'd been confused and upset – this, too, had been recorded in the notes – and apparently they'd been unsure what she meant, quite, but of course (I say 'of course' because I might have felt the same) alarm bells about Keeley had begun ringing – and the person who'd interviewed Courtney had been anxious for clarification.

There had already been concerns that, as the oldest (and a pretty girl), Keeley herself might well have been regularly abused by the drug dealers – this man included – who profited from her mother's addiction. There was no evidence of abuse, because Keeley had always refused to speak to anyone about it (perhaps, I mused, because she was old enough to understand the potential consequences of sharing anything with the official-looking women who were in and out of her mother's life) but the possibility that her mother had allowed her to be had already been discussed.

I read on, painting a picture that I really hoped I wouldn't. A picture of a girl who might well have been sexually abused for years, and by a series of men. And I didn't doubt that was what went through the minds of whoever was responsible for sorting out the mess, because if she *had* been sexually abused from a young age, there was a fair chance she might be sexually inappropriate around her younger siblings. No point wishing otherwise – I knew that. Because it was something that happened all the time.

But had it in this case? And would it in the future? It seemed not at all clear. Keeley – then just ten – had already been questioned about the night they'd been taken and, raging against everyone, wanting only to be back with her family, she had refused to say anything about it. So they tried again, anxious to piece together her role in what happened, because so much depended on that one central question. And eventually persistence bore fruit. It was all there in the records.

'Your sister said that you were holding the door while it was happening,' went the question. 'Keeley, *were* you?'

'No,' she'd said. 'No, I wasn't there!' She'd apparently said it several times, too. But eventually, perhaps sick of the endless inquisition, she'd apparently screamed that all right, yes, she *was* there, and that of *course* she'd been holding the door shut. 'I had to!' she'd told them. 'It's my job to!'

The social worker questioning her had apparently then asked, 'So it was your job to watch, was it? To watch and guard the door when the man came?'

And Keeley had apparently confirmed it.

* * *

'Did you know about all this?' I asked Danny, as early as was appropriate the following morning. I was keen to get hold of him in the window of opportunity between him getting to work and Keeley waking from her lengthy slumbers. I just couldn't stop trying to answer my own question. Guard it against whom? The nosy neighbour? Keeley's off-her-face mother? The police?

'Yes, of course,' Danny said, seemingly surprised that I even felt the need to bring it up. 'Didn't you?'

'No,' I said. 'EDT didn't have all this, did they? That's why I've been so keen to get my hands on Keeley's full records. Seriously, Danny, she has absolutely no idea why she was separated from her brothers and sisters. Did you know that?'

There was a pause. Possibly pregnant. 'Of course,' he said again.

'But you've never discussed it with her?'

'No, of course not ...' He paused again, possibly weighing up what kind of woman he was dealing with. 'There was no question of my doing so,' he went on.

'But why?' I said, still not understanding.

'Because what was the point?' he said. 'It's not as if it was ever going to change anything, was it?' Another pause. I waited. He eventually spoke again. 'I think the feeling was – still is – that we should let sleeping dogs in that department lie. After all, as I say – and I think the feeling has always been this, to be honest – that it's not as if we can *help* Keeley by going back over any of this, is it? And to lay it bare to her that she herself was the reason ... well, that's only going to make her feel even worse about herself, isn't it? Assuming that's even possible …'

He let it hang. And I stood there and weighed things up too. And thought back to two children we'd fostered before – the elder of which (in fact, both of which) had been similarly abused over several years. They too had been separated. To break the abuse cycle. To put it behind them. And, in that case, hand on heart, I realised I couldn't argue. It had been the right decision. Perhaps it had been the right decision for Keeley too.

So I finally had my answer. And it settled things in my mind a bit more. Depressingly, it also put the phone sex into perspective. For a teen who, as a little girl, had been systematically abused by strange men, what she did on the phone for money must feel like water off a duck's back. As if *she* was calling the shots. A kind of payback.

And Danny was right. I couldn't change her past. Only help her with her future. It made me even more deter-mined to see beyond the stroppy fifteen-year-old I was currently dealing with, and remember the frightened, abused ten-year-old beneath.

If sympathetic, Mike was also pragmatic. I'd droned on at him about it all as soon as I'd had the opportunity, but though he understood what I was saying he took the same view as Danny. How could it help Keeley psychologically to have chapter and verse on the reasons why she'd been separated from her siblings? It was all so much water under the bridge now, after all.

And I put it behind me, because they were both right. Did Keeley need any more reasons to feel bad about herself? No. She had enough of those already. But it galvanised me to the extent that I felt even more compelled to try and help her. To the extent that within the week I'd moved mountains for her. Well, various small heaps of educational red tape (challenging enough). And I eventually managed to sweet-talk my old colleague and friend Gary Clarke to offer Keeley a place on the Reach for Success programme that, as behaviour manager at the local comprehensive in my former life, I had helped set up.

Gary was the child protection officer there, and with Danny's grateful sanction and help had enough clout to push it through. So it was that, anxious to seize the initiative, I drove Keeley up for an interview with him as soon as the following Wednesday, where he did an impressive bit of sweet-talking too – and putting not only two days of hair and beauty on the educational table, but also having her agree to a further two half-days – one to brush up on her English and the other to work on her maths. It would be unlikely to get her remotely close to GCSE-sitting level, but that wasn't the point. It was something to put on a CV, to show that despite difficult circumstances she had at least been trying to better herself – a point he was able to get across to her so much better than I could. I could have kissed him. I definitely hugged him.

The key thing was that this wasn't anything like school, being much more like the sort of college course she'd be able to access this time next year. The Reach for Success programme was delivered off-site, free of uniforms, to pacify the most hardy school refuseniks. And it was very much centred around adult-style learning, and focused on learning job-centred skills. And when I drove Keeley up there for her first induction half-day, before she began proper, I was pleased to see it wasn't just surviving; it was thriving – it was bigger and better attended than it had ever been.

I know some people might see that as a failing by society. Quite apart from the fact that it might seem that – with their freedoms to dress as they chose, and the informal approach there – they were being rewarded for not toeing the school line. Wouldn't it be better if all school-aged children were in school? Wasn't this evidence of greater numbers failing to thrive in education?

I'd heard all the arguments, but those of us who worked in the social sector knew all too well that to see it like this was to miss the point. There were far too many kids who, like Keeley, were persistent non-attenders, and who, once they reached an age where they were deemed not worth hounding (or their parents worth prosecuting, more pragmatically), simply slipped out of sight and, as a consequence, out of the range of help and support, which meant they were much more likely to be problem adults down the line.

No, the more we could identify and mop up, and actually teach *something*, the better for everyone, as far as I could see.

And Keeley was apparently as enthused about it as I was. I was still pinching myself that she'd acquiesced to my ideas so readily – it was such a turnaround from her 'leave me alone, I'm going my own way' stance, after all, and I was still ready for it to all go 'tits up' – as Tyler might put it if out of earshot. But, for now, at least, Keeley seemed totally on board with it.

'It's not a *bit* like school, Casey,' she had enthused when I picked her up again. 'I can't believe no one ever suggested me doing something like this before. Everyone's, like, *so* cool.'

I privately wondered about how much her and my interpretation of the word 'cool' differed in this context. After all, in my day, most of the 'students' were the ones the school mostly despaired of – the trouble-makers, the bullies, the self-proclaimed no-hopers (even if I refused to believe that of them), and the angry and chronically disenchanted.

But be that as it may, the fact that she liked the look of them made it so much more likely she'd give it a good go. 'Oh, and Gary says hi,' she added. Gary had been one of the ones doing the induction. 'Can you believe that? We're actually allowed to call the teachers by their first names? And they're just so *nice*. So totally not in your face.'

Since people 'not being in her face' was such a big deal to Keeley I did a little mental fist pump at this news. And the rest of the family, having already sensed a touch of battle fatigue in me and Mike over the previous couple of weeks, were equally enthused.

Well, to a point. Keeley was due to attend her first hair and beauty session the following Monday, and though Lauren and Riley had agreed to come over to be hair models over the weekend in order to allow her to practise, Tyler was a little more reticent.

'You seriously think I'm going to let you loose on my gorgeous mop? You're having a laugh, you are, trust me,' he assured her, as the salon party gathered on the Saturday morning. 'You've not even had a single lesson yet!'

Keeley snorted at this, and, ever the quick thinker, countered with typical acuity. 'Well, that's debatable,' she said. 'It's not like that gorgeous mop of yours seems to have girls falling all over you, does it?'

Tyler narrowed his eyes, and looked decidedly piqued, but, refusing to be beaten, he soon rallied again. 'Like *you'd* know,' he quipped sharply. 'For your information, plenty of girls like my hair just the way it is, thanks – something you'd have spotted if you actually *went* to school.'

I exchanged a glance with Lauren and Riley, who were struggling to hide their grins. There was no malice to be seen. It was just the sort of pretend-tetchy banter Ty and Keeley had begun to exchange on a daily basis. 'Like cat and dog sometimes,' I observed, as Keeley chased him out of the kitchen brandishing a tail comb.

The girls were all ready for action (Mike, David and Kieron having been assembled for the occasion and detailed to take the grandkids to football) and were both at the dining table, with hair washed and towels wrapped round their heads. I tapped Riley on the shoulder. 'It's like you and flipping Kieron all over again.'

The girls now exchanged a look between themselves. Which I saw. 'What?' I said.

'Er, not *quite* like that, mother,' Riley said, grinning at her sister-in-law.

'Like what, then?' I said, fearing I knew what might be coming, even as I was in dogged denial.

Riley tutted. 'Mum, *surely* you can see it? Me and Lauren have only been here half an hour, and, *seriously?* You honestly can't see it?'

I knew exactly what she meant, and my heart sank. 'Oh, stop it, Riley,' I said (still feeling dogged). 'You're imagining things. I mean, I know Tyler was a bit in awe of her initially – God help us – and she's a pretty girl, so that's understandable. But not any more. He's well over that now. But her sweet on *him*? No way. Yes, I have to admit, a couple of weeks ago I thought that maybe he was a bit drawn to her, but no, that was just him being a boy, being around a pretty teenage girl. It's fine, he's over all that now.'

Lauren shook her head. 'He's really not, Casey,' she said. 'Riley's right. Just watch them. And it's not just Tyler, either. Keeley's just the same, whatever you say. Proper flirting. Listen to her giggling in there!'

I glanced into the living room, were they were darting round the furniture in their mutual quest to mess up each other's hair. 'Hardly flirting,' I suggested, but there was really no denying it; and I probably didn't need Riley and Lauren's 'Come *on*, Mum!' to hammer home the point. Our new 'homebody-off-to-college' version of a previously distant, shut-down Keeley was making her mark in more ways than one. Food for thought. And definitely cause for vigilance.

'I reckon you should have a quiet word with Ty, Mum,' suggested Riley. 'Don't you? Just to make it clear that she's moving on. And that while she's here she's out of bounds. He'll get that. He knows the score with her, doesn't he?'

That she's dabbled in paid-for phone sex, I thought grimly. *Yes, he does.* But not this morning of all mornings, please.

Riley grinned at Lauren. 'Bless her, she's so innocent,' she said.

'No I'm not,' I huffed. 'And stop trying to stress me out, okay? I'll deal with it – if it even turns out to be an "it" – as and when. Meanwhile, let's get this salon open for business. Keeley! You're needed!' I shouted. 'And Tyler, if you're adamant you're not up for modelling, you can go and do some revision till Denver comes over. Right, come on,' I said, waving a hand over the array of rollers, tongs, hair-dryers and straighteners we'd laid out. 'Oh, and even better news. Riley's giving you free rein over her make-up bag, so you do the whole hog – have them looking proper belles of the ball. For a change,' I added, before ducking, sharpish.

We spent the rest of that Saturday in welcome good spirits, and for the first time since Keeley had come to live with us. And in the end we made a day of it, as Mike, Tyler and Denver – who was equally resistant to having his hair interfered with – went off to help Kieron decorate his spare bedroom, heroically taking all the little ones along too.

So a fun girly day couldn't help but ensue – one in which I finally learned how to turn around the camera on my phone and take 'selfies'.

And, true to her promise (make that 'threat'), after her induction the previous day, Keeley gave me the works. I'd never had so much different make-up on all at once, much to Riley's amusement. 'I dare you to go out like that for your birthday, Mum,' she teased. 'If Dad would be seen dead with you, that is!'

With everything that had been going on lately, my birthday had been the last thing on my mind. And wouldn't have been the first thing on my mind in any year, these days, except the biggies – and as this wasn't one of them, I wasn't that bothered. After all, when you get to my age it's increasingly a trade-off – between the fun of a party as set against the stark reminder that you are a whole year older than you were before.

'It's my birthday soon too,' Keeley said, as she finished off Lauren's manicure. And it struck me that she'd said it in a different spirit than before too. Less of the 'I'm sixteen soon, *so* …' and some stark pronouncement or other, but as any teenager might at the prospect of a special day.

Except this one wouldn't be special, because it couldn't help but involve a similar trade-off. Between cherished freedom (well, Keeley's take on freedom, anyway) and the realisation that she didn't have a family with whom to share it. Once again, the vulnerable abused child took precedence in my mind over the difficult teenager. 'Then we should do something, shouldn't we?' I heard myself saying.

'Yes, let's, Mum,' Riley said – she was a good-time girl through and through. Where I always joked I had fostering antennae, Riley's were definitely more like deeley-bobbers. 'How about a little parteeeeey maybe?' she went on. 'A joint one, perhaps? We need to do *something*.'

'I'll think about it,' I promised, already knowing we probably would. After all, we were trying to keep positive, weren't we? And what better way to extend the hand of trust and hope to Keeley than to make her birthday part of my own special day?

'Oh, go on then,' I said. 'Let's. Well, once I've run it by Dad first, obviously.' And Keeley's answering smile was all the confirmation I needed to convince me it was the right thing to do.

There's a fine line between positivity and naïvety, however, and if it's one that's worth teetering across so you don't become negative and cynical, I should still have perhaps been more realistic about such progress as we'd made.

Monday morning sold me a dummy, because it went like clockwork, with Keeley fairly skipping off through the entrance to the Reach for Success centre; so keen to get in there that my words of reassurance – about not worrying about it seeming strange, and reminding her to make use of the student counsellors if she needed to – mostly fell in the swirl of air that she left in her wake.

But it was a different matter when I brought her back home. The journey itself was certainly positive, in that she couldn't seem to stop enthusing about it, but we'd not been in ten minutes – Tyler had narrowly beaten us to it – when she announced that she was planning on going out straight after tea.

'To the skate park,' she explained (which was a plus, at least, I thought – in that she was supplying that informa-tion without being asked). 'If that's okay? With Gemma and Kate. They're on the same course as me.'

'Well, I suppose so,' I said, even though she wasn't exactly asking permission, nor, strictly speaking, did she need to. Hadn't I been told that often enough? 'But you've got college again tomorrow,' I pointed out. 'So I'd like you in by 8 p.m. latest, okay?'

She was about to pull a face but I watched her think better of it. 'Okay,' she said, slipping off the coat she'd be donning again an hour later. 'Oh, and by the way, I've invited them to our birthday party. If that's okay, of course,' she added sweetly.

'She did *what*?' Mike asked, once he was home. Keeley had, by now, already left. 'I hope you said something, Case. We don't know anything about them! They can't just show up here. Not with all the little ones coming. I don't like this at all.'

Since he'd not liked the idea of hosting a joint birthday party in the first place – 'asking for trouble, at her age' being his not unreasonable opinion – I didn't want to push it.

'I tell you what, I'll see if I can get them round after college one day,' I reassured him. 'See if they have any horns hidden under their hair … Seriously, though, love, I'm sure they're perfectly nice girls. Got to be better than the wasters she mooches around town with. At least they're *doing* something.'

Mike's look didn't need to be accompanied by any words. How many times had I come home with hair-raising tales about some of the little 'angels' we had at the centre down the years? Way too many. Perhaps that had been a mistake.

But further discussion about the desirability of holding a party in the first place was soon superseded by more pressing concerns about the here and now. Eight o'clock came and went, and all too soon became eight thirty, swiftly followed by nine and nine thirty as well. I had texted Keeley twice and received no replies, either – and this despite this being one of the house rules we'd discussed more than once. Her phone went straight to voicemail as well.

'This is just *too* much!' Mike seethed, his mood now hovering between dark and black. 'Her first bloody day at college and she goes out and does this to us. She'd better have a damn good excuse ... Scrub that. I'm not accepting *any* excuse. This is not carrying on again. Not a chance.'

'I could run to the skate park,' Tyler offered, and I could see he was as anxious about Keeley's fall from grace back to disgrace as much as I was. Could leopards ever change their spots when they were grown? Perhaps not. 'Shall I do that?' he persisted, while Mike stared out of the window, up the road. 'She might just have lost track of time again.'

'No you won't, son,' Mike said, lowering the curtain he'd been holding up. 'I shall drive there. And when I find her she'll be getting a piece of my mind. This is it, love, I mean it,' he added to me, reaching for his car keys. 'You know what we said.'

I saw Tyler looking anxiously across at me. 'I know,' I said glumly. 'But please don't go off on one, Mike. Let's deal with it calmly, yes? We don't want her running off and everything just going from bad to worse.'

'Bad to worse?' Mike's look was stony, his feelings about Keeley clear. 'You honestly think I care that much? You honestly think that's not a risk I'm prepared to take?'

And when he shut the door behind him he did it too quietly.

Too precisely. As if in danger of slamming it otherwise.

He meant what he said, I knew.

'Dad doesn't like Keeley, does he?' Tyler said.

Chapter 10

As it turned out, the whole débâcle had, thankfully, been something of an anti-climax.

Mike had intercepted Keeley not ten minutes into his drive to the skate park, already weaving her unsteady way home.

Neither of us had the appetite for an interrogation then, either. For one thing it was a school night and way past Tyler's bedtime. And for another, with Keeley squiffy, if not paralytic (thankfully), there was no point in trying to get any sense out of her anyway. It was sufficient that she was glum-faced and contrite rather than defiant, and only too happy to be sent straight to bed.

And – well, well, well – here she was this morning, up at the crack of dawn, all ready for college, and chock-full of heartfelt apologies. She was clearly anxious to break down the wall of distrust Mike had now assembled – as he'd already made clear to me, very grumpily, the night before.

And, give her credit, she was doing her level best to make a highly dubious-sounding story work, all about some supposed-alcohol-free-but-wasn't cider.

'We *really* didn't realise, honestly!' she entreated, for about the third time since she'd surprised us in the kitchen with a virtual dawn chorus of appeasement gestures, including busily clearing away the plates Mike and I had left on the table, like a supercharged Snow White.

I knew Mike was a great deal less inclined than me to even listen, but he at least gave her benefit of appearing to. Which he could afford to. He'd soon be off to work, and able to leave me to it, wouldn't he?

'Please say you believe me,' she said, turning her eyes on him particularly. 'Why wouldn't we believe her?' The 'her' in question being some new mate from the course she had 'mistakenly' trusted to tell the truth. 'I mean, it looked completely legit. And it was fruit cider. You know the kind. With a picture of a bunch of cranberries on it and everything. Why *wouldn't* we believe her?'

'Because you didn't come down in the last shower of rain, perhaps?' I suggested.

'But it was *dark*,' she threw in, causing Mike to roll his eyes. 'I couldn't read the back of the can even if I wanted to.'

'Even more reason not to drink it,' I pointed out.

'But she told us it was *fine*,' she persisted. 'So why wouldn't we believe her? It was only when I'd drank two cans of the stuff that it dawned on me. So, I mean, it's not like I was drinking booze on purpose, is it? I didn't even *know*. It's like ... it's like ... it's like I was almost violated!'

Quite apart from the ridiculous picture she was painting – of this random girl, running a mobile branch of the local booze shop, dispensing dubious cans of strong cider – her choice of word made me laugh out loud. Violated? Where had she dredged that one up? Violated, by fruity cider? She really was quite the drama queen. I had to give her that. Even if she was trying to take us for utter mugs.

'Okay,' I said, having already decided to keep a cool head and run with it. 'So then what? How did you go from, um, being *forced* to consume alcohol, to wandering the streets at ten o'clock at night, when you were meant to be home?'

Keeley shook her head as if in disbelief. 'Well, *duh*!' she said, shaking her head in apparent astonishment. 'We were *drunk* by then, weren't we? We didn't know what we were doing.' She glanced at Mike, then looked at me. 'Casey, honestly, you mean *you've* never been drunk?'

Thankfully, Tyler appeared in the kitchen just as the question had been asked. Which both saved me from having to engage further in such a silly discussion and provided a timely pause, before Mike left for work.

'Well, Keeley,' he said, adopting her own style. 'As you might say, *whatever*. Whatever the reason, I told you last night that your actions have consequences, and, guess what – they're here. You come straight home from college tonight. No hanging around with friends. You can have a night at home for once, about which I don't expect you to argue. And if you do – either to me now, or to Casey later on, tonight's night in will be extended to a week in. You understand.'

'*What?*' Keeley gasped. 'You mean I'm grounded? But I apologised!'

Mike nodded. 'Yes, you have. And we've accepted your apology.' He reached for his coat and began putting it on. 'And just as I and Casey have done that, so *you* should accept the result of your actions graciously. Think on it. Chalk it up to experience. If you then learn from your mistakes – that's the point, here – and make a *different* choice next time, then you will have actually *proved* that you're sorry, won't you? It won't just be empty words. So let's see,' he said sternly. 'A night at home won't kill you, anyway.'

Mike kissed me and Tyler goodbye and left, leaving Keeley with her mouth open and a bit of an atmosphere, which Tyler was quick to try and lighten. 'Porridge and syrup, anyone?' he asked, smiling as he held out a bunch of sachets. 'Lots of syrup. Though I reckon it's a bit late to try and sweeten Dad up.'

He then smiled, clearly pleased to see Keeley's frown turn to a grin.

'You should go on the stage, you,' she said, batting him on the arm. 'And go on, then, O King of the Microwave. I'll join you. But don't blame your dad. I know I'm pretty high maintenance.'

Hmm, I thought. Spoken like a woman of the world. 'Glad you've noticed,' I said, deciding there was no point in being off with her. As Mike had made clear, the ball was in her court now. To follow up her words with appropriate action. Which she either would or wouldn't do. I hoped she would.

'And like Mike said,' I went on, 'a night at home won't kill you. So when you see your friends today make sure they know that, okay? In fact, it wouldn't hurt if you showed willing by staying in a bit more anyway, love. If you want to do your best at college you are going to need your sleep.'

Keeley nodded contritely. 'But they're still good for the party at the weekend, right?'

Ah. The party. Well, the 'party' in inverted commas really, given that, apart from Keeley's new friends, it was going to consist of just the family, essentially, plus Denver (of course) and, if they felt up to it, my elderly mum and dad. Though I had at least come around to the idea of the two girls from college coming, as it would make it more fun for the youngsters.

Though not *too* much fun, I thought, mentally filing the previous night's shenanigans. 'That's a thought,' I said. 'I trust the girl who foisted the alcohol upon you so scurrilously isn't one of the ones you've invited, Keeley.'

'*God*, no,' she assured me. 'She's a complete hoe.'

Tyler's splutter of amusement wasn't lost on me. In reality, I knew it was unlikely that she even existed. Keeley was more than capable of knowing cider from Ribena, after all. Still, again, I ran with it.

'Good. And, yes, provided that you settle down and do as we've asked you, they can come. But I can promise you that if there's another incident between now and then the whole thing will be cancelled. Understood?'

Keeley saluted and grinned at Tyler as he passed her a bowl of porridge. 'Aye aye, captain,' she said. 'Message received and understood.'

Received, yes, I thought. We'd have to wait and see about the rest.

Whether because she was super-sorry or just super-shrewd, Keeley's behaviour over the next few days was exemplary. On her actual birthday we celebrated with a family meal at home, at which it seemed almost possible, according to Mike, anyway, that the real Keeley been taken by aliens in the night, and replaced with a trained replicant, such a vision of mannered loveliness was she.

The day had also brought presents. Presents from all of us, of course – new trainers, a silver locket, a scarf and gloves set, a retro sweet tin – and she'd also been given gifts by her new best friends, Gemma and Katy from college, which made me feel much better disposed towards them. And, slightly bizarrely, to my mind, a card and TopShop voucher from Steve and Zoe Burke – the last thing in the world I would have expected. But perhaps Keeley's foster sister Jade had been involved. They couldn't see each other, but the bond was clearly still strong between them.

'Guilt money,' Keeley said darkly, as she prised the plastic card off to check the amount. 'But money's money, eh? *Very* happy to spend this.'

And soon the weekend rolled around and the party was upon us and, like anyone anywhere who's had a trouble-free week, I was not only looking forward to it, but, given the Keeley we'd been seeing over recent stress-free days, didn't so much as devote a second to contemplating how things might go wrong.

Which made me doubly cross with myself when they did.

The evening, without question, had been a success. All the family round, my elderly mum and dad included, and defying their years by being the ones doing the most dancing to the eighties playlist I'd so carefully constructed. The house was rammed – so much for the modest gathering I'd first mooted, with both relatives and friends and a few of our party-minded neighbours – spilling out everywhere, with the usual high-decibel nucleus in the kitchen.

And, as young people tend to when at multi-generational gatherings, the youngsters at ours had immediately formed their own clique, with their HQ in the fairy-lit conservatory.

And more fool me for not worrying what they might be up to. I was lost in conversation with my sister Donna in the living room when Kieron came up and yanked on my dress sleeve. He looked worried. 'Mum, I think you'd best go check on Tyler,' he whispered. 'If I'm right, he's been drinking. Or he's taken something,' he added, lowering his voice further. 'Him *and* Denver. They're both acting really odd.'

Tyler? Taken something? That I definitely couldn't believe. He was no angel – and I didn't come down in the last shower of rain, either – but doing that, at a party, at home, with us all there? With my *mum and dad* there? That I *wouldn't* believe. But drinking? Perhaps. Kieron hardly touched alcohol. It 'upset his brain' was how he'd put it when he'd tried it. He wasn't teetotal, but he was certainly no boozer, so he'd be bound to be concerned.

'I'm sure you're wrong, love,' I told him as I followed him through the house. 'He might be daft at times, but he's not stupid. Probably just high spirits – that and having the girls here – which is making both boys a bit silly. If he'd wanted a beer, which is *fine*, he'd have asked Mike or me for one.'

So much for Mrs Confident About Everything.

Because one look into the conservatory, where all five youngsters were still gathered, proved me wrong. Tyler and Denver had indeed been drinking, and a good deal more than one drink apiece, by the look of them: they were both sprawled on my wicker sofa, giggling like ten-year-olds.

I thought instantly, and anxiously, of cannabis, seeing that. Perhaps Kieron had been right after all. But I'd have smelt it, and couldn't – and I had a good nose for it after years working in a school. No, they were just giggling because they were silly teenage boys, being dangled on a string by three street-wise, sassy girls, at least one of whom chatted up grown men (to put it politely) for pocket money.

My gaze naturally moved to the three girls in question, who were gathered by the doors into the garden, each with a wine bottle in their hands. As in a whole bottle apiece, and all were more than half empty, and, to my utter astonishment, all the girls were smoking as well. Yes, they were making a vague effort to blow their smoke outside. But they were still smoking in my conservatory. Indoors.

Couldn't be bothered to actually *go* outside. They were smoking in my house.

Which, respect-wise, was the biggest slap in the face of all. Not because they were doing something they knew they shouldn't – a zillion teenagers have done similarly when their parents have been away – but because they were doing it knowing full well that our whole family were in the house. Setting me up as the gullible idiot they so obviously thought me to be.

'You three!' I barked. 'Put those cigarettes out right now!'

I glared at Keeley's friends, then. And gestured to the wine bottles. 'Did you two bring those?'

'Oh, Chrrrrist!' Keeley drawled drunkenly. 'Here we go.' She let the words hang for long enough to make it clear to her new buddies that I had previous in the business of being an old bag. 'We are all six*teen*!' she snapped back at me. 'In case you hadn't noticed. And you're not their mother. Or *my* mother, for that fact. *Chrrrrist*. We're just having a bloody drink. What's the big deal?'

Her prettiness had disappeared completely. And her eyes, which were reddening, challenged me so forcefully it was almost as if she was willing me to hit her, and I had to quash an urge to slap her cheek for that. I balled my fists. 'Not in my bloody house, you aren't,' I said instead, before marching across to Tyler, who was gazing at me dozily from under half-closed eyelids. 'And what do you think you two are doing?' I asked, planting my fists on my hips now. 'Why would you *do* this, Ty?'

Tyler hiccupped before answering. Then looked sheepish. 'I dunno,' he said, slurring the words. 'But it's not her fault, Mum, seriously.' Except he couldn't manage 'seriously'. Only 'sirrrush-ush-ush', which caused Denver to collapse into another fit of giggles. Which then sent Ty off again as well.

God, I thought miserably, *give me strength*.

I turned around. Kieron was still standing in the door-way behind me. 'Love,' I said, 'can you get these two up to Ty's bedroom for me, please? And call Denver's mum for me? Let her know he'll be sleeping over? The pull-out's made up. Put him on that.'

'With absolute pleasure,' Kieron said, making it clear as he did so that he intended it to be one – and that he wasn't exactly planning on being gentle with them either. He was a kind soul, my Kieron, but I could see he was angry – upset, more than anything, that the boys had let me down.

'Make sure they both drink some water,' I added, as he hauled them up and frogmarched them back through the kitchen. The three girls meanwhile just stood and watched this, looking bored. It took me straight back to my days dealing with the difficult kids in school.

'So, ladies,' I said, feeling my anger welling further, 'now to deal with *you*. I am –'

'I don't fucking *think* so,' Keeley interrupted, with such bile that it made me wince, as she reached into her hand-bag for her packet of cigarettes. 'Come on, girls,' she said, gesturing with a nod that they should follow. 'Let's fuck off outta this shit-hole, yeah? I'm up to here –' she touched her forehead and looked at me again pointedly. 'Up to *here* with the bloody goody-goody act, seriously.'

She then made to pass me, to go inside. And then, presumably, out – the new, improved Keeley having already disappeared.

'Don't you dare leave this house,' I warned, blocking her with my arm. 'You've been drinking and are not in a fit state to be off wandering the bloody streets. I mean it, Keeley,' I said, dropping my arm again to test her. I expected her to move, but, thankfully, she stayed put. 'I'm telling you now,' I said coldly, 'if you defy me and leave I'll have no alternative but to call the police.'

This seemed to decide her – she actually sneered, and I felt my heart sink. What the hell should I have said instead? 'Good luck with that,' she said, making a cutesy bye-bye sign with her hand as she ushered the girls past me. 'You think they'll care? I'm *sixteen*.' She rolled her eyes. 'They'll just laugh at you.'

And then she was gone. So were her lovely new friends. And my Tyler and Denver were drunk and being put to bed. And I now had to go out and face all those faces. All those sympathetic looks from my well-meaning family. And – a dead cert – a *very* pointed one from Mike. Happy, happy birthday to me.

How does the song go? The one about it being a party and being allowed to cry if I wanted to.

That was the one. I sat down, and I did.

Chapter 11

As a foster carer, it's good practice not to leap before looking. To try, wherever possible, to mentally count to ten, and to take stock of a situation before reacting to it. To take time to break down all the seemingly insignificant actions that ultimately led to the current crisis, whatever kind of crisis it might be.

Over the years, taking stock before acting had become second nature; not necessarily at the time – not always possible in the heat of an angry moment – but certainly as soon as possible after the event, and before taking any precipitous action, or, most importantly, making over-emotional entries in my log.

There was an exception to this, however, and that was during the first couple of weeks of any long-term placement, when I'd use my log almost as a personal diary and commit to it as reactively as I felt.

During this period, as well as recording all the things you'd expect – such as 'a good day today for A', or 'B got up on time and without fuss' or 'discovered that C doesn't eat breakfast, and has been hiding food in their room' – I also include all my own thoughts and feelings and frustrations, so I have a clear record not just of the child's emotional state, but also how *the two of us* are getting on, as well as a fuller picture of the daily routine. I turn every happening of note into a little story.

The reason for doing this is simple. Life as a foster carer can often be so hectic that the really important things can easily be missed. The little things said, the little flashpoints that might have happened, the moments when a child's psyche was suddenly exposed in an all-too-brief glimpse. Such insights into a child can so easily be lost in the white noise of adjustment and settling in; all potentially valuable pieces of the complex jigsaw that can get lost forever.

And though John and various social workers know it's one of my little idiosyncrasies, I don't do it just to please myself. It also has the potential to give future carers something more tangible to go on than just a series of detached-sounding reports.

Finally, of course, it helps the child, too. If some insight into their make-up can travel with them – bad or good – others caring for them can hopefully care for them all the better, adapting more readily to the real child behind the mask.

I'm not sure how long I sat in the conservatory snivelling, only that I'd just about dried them when my eyes saw a space where a pot plant should be. It wasn't anything grand. Just an orchid from a supermarket, almost all the flowers dropped now. But it had been a present from my oldest grandchild, Levi, back in the summer, and he'd been at great pains to tell me, having looked it all up on Google, that if I hung on to it, only watering it very, very sparingly, it should at some point grow a new crop of blooms.

Yet it was missing. And a short investigation soon revealed that someone at some point had knocked it off the little side table. It was now lying on its side, half out of the pot, in the corner.

I picked it up and, though it bore no obvious scars (orchids are pretty tough buggers, after all), just the fact of it having been swept away, even if unwittingly, set me off feeling sorry for myself all over again. Did I really have the mental energy or the will to deal with Keeley? She was beginning to really rile me – one minute all sweetness and supplication and sorrys and the next throwing it back into our faces. And she'd been horrible, truly horrible, when drunk. Really nasty. A phrase came to me. *In vino veritas*?

Which was true of almost *all* kids in the care system, my good self hurried in to tell my tired self. I'd dealt with far worse and for far longer. But my tired self kept peddling the same line, over and over. Keeley *was* sixteen now, and perhaps the consensus about her was right; that she was probably beyond the kind of help we could offer.

Perhaps I should take her at her word, too, and simply leave her to roam the streets. Report it, yes, of course. Alert EDT, obviously. But leave any police involvement, or otherwise, to them. Go to bed, in short, and leave her and her cronies to it. As she had also pointed out, I wasn't her mother.

And for a while that was exactly what I did. I blew my nose, I emerged, we all made light of Keeley's adolescent 'flounce', and everyone was quick to reassure me – from Mum and Dad down to my grown-up niece Chloe – that it was no more than typical sixteen-year-old behaviour. That Ty and Denver would both be pretty sheepish come the morning – by which time, of course, Keeley would have long since come home and gone to bed, having grown cold, having run out of phone signal or wanting food.

But I'm not one for waiting around for things to happen, and there was no way in the world that either Mike or I could go to bed. So once the house was quiet and still – and Mike had gallantly agreed to do the remaining clearing up – I went and got my laptop, and went back into the conservatory, threw a blanket around my shoulders and tried to get my head straight.

Mike, predictably, was a mixture of natural concern and justifiable anger. He'd already run through what he planned on doing, which was to completely re-establish and strengthen the boundaries, and if Keeley didn't like it – or, indeed, stick to it – he wanted to make clear that she was welcome to move on somewhere else.

I knew he meant it as well. Sixteen was a million miles from eleven or twelve in terms of what role we as foster carers could play. Not if that role was being repeatedly rejected. 'So if she wants to keep living with us,' he'd added, 'then *everything* needs to change. Her choice, love.'

As indeed it was. And she was on extremely thin ice. He laid the blame for Tyler and Denver's behaviour at Keeley's feet too. Which was fair enough again. Yet, reasonable though it was – and I knew no one would judge us – I just kept coming back to my default position, that the key to helping Keeley lay in further unpeeling the layers and getting to grips with the little abandoned girl within. The little abandoned *abused* child.

So I sat and read – there was nothing much else to do while we waited. (And wait we would; though he'd offered I didn't want Mike driving round the streets like a kerb-crawler, looking for her again.) I read all the correspondence between John and me, and the emails exchanged with Danny. I read through all the attachments again – the important information that always filtered through at the start of a new placement, in this case Keeley's school records (scant now), further information about her birth family (very little) and a few notes about her previous placement plans, which told me nothing I didn't already know.

Then, finally, having learned nothing new of note, I went back to my own daily log sheets, so I could revisit the early days after her arrival:

Day four [though every log was dated, I always worked like this – from arrival day to whenever]. When Keeley finally emerged from her bedroom it was almost noon and she was in a foul mood. I tried my best to cheer her up but the more I tried, the worse her behaviour became. I was feeling really stressed by this point as we didn't seem to be making any headway, or at the very least, taking one step forward and two steps back. I yelled back at her to go back upstairs (cross with myself for yelling – she always seems to be able to goad me into yelling back at her – shouldn't happen!) and to come down when her mood had improved. She then turned to the fireplace and spent some time with her back to me, apparently looking at all the photographs on the mantelpiece. Then, without warning, she picked one up and hurled it across the room – not towards me, thankfully – smashing the glass and damaging the frame. I struggled to keep my temper – not least because it was the one the kids had given me for Mother's Day, of all the grandkids, and the fact that it was a gift made it doubly infuriating. I went to chastise her – sternly but calmly (a lot more calmly than I felt!) – but she barged past me and ran upstairs, yelling profanities at me all the way. I really can't say at this point if the placement is going to last. It feels harsh to be saying so this early on, but I'm not sure it's working. *Nothing* seems to be working.

I looked at the entry again, remembering the scene and the day. I remembered feeling furious and then, uncharacteristically, even tearful, as I'd picked up the shards of glass and gathered them into the dustpan, and saw that some of the little diamantés in the frame had fallen out.

I remembered too that I looked into the faces of my four grandchildren and had one of those thoughts every foster carer experiences from time to time, questioning whether I needed or wanted such a disruptive and negative influence in my house.

But now I revisited the scene in my mind and saw it slightly differently. Nothing had changed about it, but my perspective had begun to. How must it feel to be Keeley, seeing those happy untroubled faces smiling out at her? Seeing a mantelpiece crammed with the starkest of contrasts – evidence of the history of a functional happy family? Difficult at best. Almost as if they were all lined up there just to rub salt in her wounds. And on top of the 'rogues' gallery' she'd leafed through, so she could get to know us better ... Perhaps it just made her feel *worse*.

In truth, I could have had those thoughts then – I even might have. After all, part of our training is to always keep in mind that children aren't born evil – they are damaged by people and circumstances beyond their control. And many a child had lashed out in my living room before that. It went with the career choice. But now I thought about the picture she'd chosen to take out her anger on and it suddenly seemed such a deliberate choice. My four grand-children, her four siblings. An emotional kick in the teeth if ever there was one. That was so obviously the photo-graph she would choose. God, they were even almost matched in age!

I was deep in my reverie, reading on, trying to see between the lines of type, when a sound heralded Mike popping his head around the door. 'All done,' he said. 'So, what's the plan going to be with madam? It's gone one.'

I could see he'd softened towards Keeley now – well, just a little. Probably just the responsible parent in him kicking in. It's one thing to know that you don't have to officially worry about an older foster child, quite another to switch off the worrying switch. Even if no one would hold us responsible if anything happened to her, what parent wouldn't feel responsible?

'I don't know,' I began, closing the lid on the laptop.

'I think I should have a drive around,' he said. 'I can't not, love. I don't suppose you know where her two friends live, do you?'

I shook my head miserably. What a crappy parent I was! I hadn't even thought to ask that. I suppose I just assumed that, given her age, I wouldn't need to know these things like that straight away. I'd barely registered them as friends, let alone knew anything about them – well, apart from their penchant for disrespect and cheap wine. I stood up and shrugged off the blanket.

'Well, I'll just have a drive around in that case,' he said.

I followed him back into the kitchen. 'And I suppose I'd better get on and phone EDT and report it. Even if you do find her, we need to make this official and get it on record, don't we?'

'And prepare for a long night ahead,' Mike said wearily. He stretched his arms above his head, then held them out towards me. 'God, I'm tired,' he said, pulling me in for a hug. 'Are we getting too old for this lark, you reckon?'

* * *

He was right, as my instinct had already told me, given the amount of wine the girls had already consumed before they'd left. And was he right about us getting too old for all this hassle? Right then, it certainly felt that way.

He headed out and I trudged off to phone EDT. The lady who answered was friendly and efficient and took down the details with calm detachment. It was a box-ticking exercise, and both of us knew it. *What time did she leave? Have you reported it to the police? Can you keep us informed if anything else happens? Will you please phone back and let us know as soon as you have a police log number?*

I answered the questions with as much enthusiasm as they'd been asked and, before hanging up, assured her that if Keeley wasn't home within the next half an hour I would get on to the police. I then went upstairs, on tired legs, to check on the boys, who were both sleeping soundly, Tyler sprawled in his bed, Denver curled up on the pull-out, looking like butter wouldn't melt. With my own bed a no-no, at least for the moment, I then wandered across the landing into Keeley's bedroom. Not to snoop around. Just to stand and survey her tiny temporary kingdom, which was chock full of her stuff – though, as ever, very tidy. Her expensive make-up, all stacked neatly in its compartmentalised Perspex tray. Her array of designer perfumes arranged in a perfect semi-circle, in front of, and reflected in, the triple mirror on her dressing table. The freshly ironed pile of branded hoodys and T-shirts, still on the tub chair, and waiting to be put away. So much stuff, and yet … I glanced around me, and thought of Tyler's room. So *little*. All this expensive stuff and yet so little emotional wealth. No family photos, no quirky snaps of her and her friends. No silly notes, no greeting cards – bar the few she'd had from us – no materially worthless but oh-so-important ticket stubs or lanyards, as Tyler had. Despite her many belongings, this room was void of anything that suggested a normal, happy teenager resided in it.

I was back downstairs, in thoughtful mood, and just debating whether to make myself another coffee and risk what little sleep I'd have time to snatch, when Mike reappeared, empty handed.

'Time to call the police, love,' he said, going across to the kettle to make the coffee decision for me. 'I don't doubt she's spark out at one of her friend's places by now, but we might as well crack on. Do you want me to do it?'

I shook my head. 'You make the coffee and I'll go and do it.' I managed a wan smile. 'And I'll see you on the other side.'

And it was as long a job as experience had long since told me it would be. A full ninety minutes of answering questions, going through a set format for dealing with situations such as this, when a vulnerable young person has gone AWOL. And despite her age, Keeley was still classed as vulnerable, which meant that the usual response – to wait until twenty-four hours had passed before acting – was replaced by a concerted effort to aid any search for her, which left me embarrassed once again as I had to confess that, bar such physical descriptions as I could manage, I didn't know the first thing about the two girls she'd gone off with. I didn't even know their surnames, let alone their addresses. I could doubtless find out, in time – a call to Gary Clarke would sort that – but it was almost two in the morning by the time we were done and they'd need more than 'three sixteen-year-old girls had flounced off' to start ringing all and sundry in the small hours. For all we knew, it was just as Mike had already predicted, that Keeley was asleep on a pull-out in someone else's home.

At 2.30 a.m. and feeling defeated, we crawled up to bed, taking our mobile phones with us – definitely not aids to restful sleep – as we waited for news, or, usually worse, a sharp knock at the door.

It was just gone 5.00 a.m. when I finally took the call. Feeling as if I'd only just drifted off, I was confused by the noise at first, but then, fearing the phone's trilling might wake Tyler and Denver, I quickly stretched out to grab it, desperately hoping it was good news.

It was. The police officer was quick to reassure us. 'We have a very tired, very cold and very contrite young lady with us,' he told me. 'And she wants to know if it's okay to come home.'

Chapter 12

With the news that Keeley was safe and being returned to us, Mike, who was bleary-eyed and doughy-faced when I woke him, turned full circle and was immediately cross again. And I got that. How many times did the average parent go through that same emotional process? Something happens, a child vanishes, some other crisis befalls them – and, as a parent, you worry yourself sick, don't you? And then, when all's well, your feelings turn on a sixpence. Worry turns to relief, and with the relief comes a jolt of anger – that they've had the audacity (or the stupidity, more often) to put you through the trauma of having to worry yourself sick in the first place. So instead of feeling better, what you mostly feel is furious. Well, at least for a little while.

'You'd better deal with her on your own,' he said, once I'd shaken him awake and given him the fuller picture. 'Or I might not be responsible for my actions. I certainly don't trust myself to stay calm.'

And I agreed with him, both privately and then verbally. And again when he reiterated what he'd said to me earlier – that perhaps we *were* getting too old for all this stress.

The policeman who'd called me turned out to be a burly thirty-something and, unbeknown to Keeley, who was on the doorstep in front of him, with a bit of a twinkle in his eye. Which was remarkable, given that it was close on six in the morning, but I recognised someone who seemed to be happy in his work, which meant it was lucky it had been him who picked her up.

He ushered Keeley in before him (she was entirely without a hint of twinkle) and while she dived into the downstairs loo he followed me into the living room, where, once he'd refused coffee or tea (he was about to go off shift), he told me, in hushed tones, in case she heard us, that I didn't need to worry because he'd read her the riot act, in no uncertain terms, and was confident he'd hammered his point home. 'We've had a fair few tears,' he added. 'And between you and me I'm not without sympathy for the lass. Seems her so-called mates weren't that matey after all.'

'Do you know what she's been up to?' I asked, keeping my voice low as well.

'Not a lot, by all accounts – well, if what's she told me is actually true. The usual hanging about aimlessly' – he mentioned a faraway park – 'well, till they hooked up with a couple of lads – deadbeats the pair of them, and both known to us, it turns out, and the four of them pretty much buggered off and left her.'

'What, the girls did?'

'It appears so. Oh, and, for future reference, Mrs Watson, one of those girls – the one called Gemma? She's known to us too. Not exactly a hardened wrong 'un, but, well, you know how it goes with these youngsters. She's in foster care herself. Bit of a silly girl. Easily led. So she certainly has the potential to be. Anyway, at least you have this one home finally, for your sins.' The toilet flushed then. 'So you can finally get off to bed at least,' he finished.

'Some hope,' I said wryly. 'But thank you *so* much. We really appreciate it.'

'No thanks necessary,' he said, as Keeley appeared in the doorway. 'For one thing it was Keeley here who found *us*, not the other way around. And' – he touched my arm – 'we're all in this together, aren't we? And just you shape up, young lady,' he added, looking sharply at Keeley. 'Do as this long-suffering lady tells you, you hear me? And remember what I said. We've got better things to be doing than acting as a taxi service. Much more *important* things to be doing. So next time we pick you up you'll be coming back to *our* accommodation for the night. Remember that.'

Keely tried out a scowl but I could see her heart wasn't in it. She looked grey and, for a moment, I thought she might throw up. *Vulnerable minor.* The official term popped into my head. 'What d'you say, Keeley?' I snapped, even though I wasn't by now feeling very snappish.

'Sorry,' she mumbled. And as her chin lifted, I saw the glint of tears tracking down her face.

Hmm. Sorry *after* the act. Again.

* * *

I sat up with Keeley for another half-hour after the police-man left. I knew Mike would be up soon, but since she was so subdued and contrite I wanted to hear for myself how the night had panned out. If what the officer had said was true, I had gained an unexpected new perspective. Far from being the cocksure, independent young woman she purported to be, was Keeley – now I'd finally observed her in the new light of peer relationships – actually suffering from a bad case of 'needing to be liked' syndrome? Were her new friends (Keeley had made much of how many friends she had since day one) actually treating her with disdain?

If I'd been unimpressed by their lack of respect in a stranger's home earlier in the evening (how was it still the same evening? My eyelids told me differently) I was doubly unimpressed by the way they'd apparently dumped her when a more exciting prospect had emerged in the shape of two apparently dodgy lads.

'It wasn't *like* that,' Keeley insisted, through a veil of snivels, sobs and tears – the stock in trade of many a miser-able sixteen-year-old girl before her. 'I just didn't wanna go with them, okay? I could have, but I didn't want to.'

'That's not what you told the policeman.'

'Yeah, well.'

'Yeah well what, Keeley?'

'Yeah well what was I supposed to say? I needed to get home, didn't I?'

'So you gave him a sob story. Said they'd dumped you. That's a very nice way to treat your friends, I must say.'

She rolled her eyes. 'Can I go to bed?'

'No, you can't, Keeley. You've kept me and Mike up all night and you can stay up a bit longer. So, how come no one was out looking for Gemma and Katie?'

'Because Gemma told her foster mum she was staying over at Katie's and Katie told her mum she was staying over at Gemma's, *obviously*.'

She was getting chippy now, trying to bat me away. But I wasn't having any of it. 'There's no "obviously" about it, Keeley. Does it occur to none of you that it's not on to carry on like that? Suppose something happens to them? You don't know these lads from Adam, do you?'

'Trust me, I don't *want* to,' she huffed. 'Look, can I just go to bed? I've said I'm sorry, haven't I?'

'Saying you're sorry isn't the universal panacea, Keeley.'

She looked at me balefully, her big eyes smudged with tears and mascara. 'Well, what *else* am I supposed to do?'

'Stop behaving like a bloody child in the first place!'

I didn't mean to swear. Not the best thing to slip out, given the amount of times I pulled her up on it. But it had popped out and I couldn't now pop it back in. But what did it matter, really? We were way past that now. 'Seriously, Keeley, it seems to me that you are determined to mess things up for yourself. It's almost like you actively *want* to push us to the limit. *Is* that what you want? For me to call Danny in the morning and ask him to have you moved on somewhere else? Yet more strangers? Because right now you're this close' – I put thumb and finger together – 'to that happening, believe me. You're sixteen now, after all, as you keep on reminding us. And if you don't want our support, then you only have to say so. Believe me, if you're that hell bent on your whole "offskies" plan, maybe we'd better put it in action right now.'

I took a couple of deep breaths. She was crying again, head down, the tears dripping into her lap. 'Love, I just want to *help* you,' I said. '*We* want to help you. And I thought you were enjoying college. Yet ...' I paused. 'Yet it seems the first thing you do is hook up with the worst kind of people. Get into scrapes. Go off AWOL. What's the attraction?' I raised a hand and touched a finger to her temple. 'What's going on up there? Keeley, I can't help you if carry on as if you don't even *want* help, can I? Look at me, Keeley. Do you want our help? *Do* you want to stay with us?'

She let out a great heaving cry then and – to my utter astonishment – fell against me heavily, burrowing into my shoulder as I put my arms around her and shaking with sobs. 'I don't *know* what I want,' she mumbled into my dressing gown, scenting the air with her expensive perfume.

Though, whatever she might want, one thing was clear, that there was something she *needed*, and that was a hug. I sat and held her for a good twenty minutes.

'Oh God,' Tyler groaned, at the kitchen table the following morning. 'Nan and Granddad must think I am such a prize prat. I should ring them to say sorry, shouldn't I, Mum? And, cross my heart and hope to die,' he said, with feeling, 'I am *never, ever* drinking again.'

I say 'next' morning. It was the same morning – *still*. Not quite noon yet. Thank God it was Saturday.

'I'm never drinking again either,' said Denver. 'Well, not till I'm eighteen, anyway, obviously,' he added sagely. 'God, I'm *so* sorry, Casey.'

I was tempted to say 'yeah, right', re the 'not till I'm eighteen' bit, because there was a slim to zero chance of *that* happening, I reckoned, even if I didn't officially know about it. But I decided to let it go. They'd learn. They *were* learning.

As was I, as it turned out. Because it had come to light that it hadn't just been beer they'd been drinking. A recce of the conservatory by Mike, before he stomped off to football in high dudgeon, had established that Keeley's 'friends' hadn't just brought wine with them. They'd been necking something called Jägermeister, and one sniff at the almost empty bottle he'd unearthed from beneath the sofa was enough to make me think I'd probably be saying that in Ty and Denver's shoes too. Quite apart from anything else – it smelled like the devil's own cough syrup – it was about 35 per cent proof. And there'd been just five of them drinking it, at most. So the maths wasn't hard.

But we'd done the post-mortem now, and as far as I was concerned that was the end of it, even if Denver still had to run the gauntlet of his mother. (As did I, to an extent, because I felt very guilty. Thank goodness she was the non-judgemental pragmatic type. 'Denver's big enough and ugly enough to know what he's doing,' had been her generous response when I kept on – and on and on – apologising.)

'Look, the pair of you messed up,' I said. 'But there's no harm done – except to your heads – so let's move on now.

You can do your penance by making the breakfast. If you can stomach any, that is.'

Apparently they could. Cast-iron stomachs, teenage boys.

Keeley, on the other hand, wasn't about to get off so lightly. She didn't yet know it, and perhaps wouldn't at any point, but had what to do about her been Mike's decision alone, that phone call to Danny would already have been made. As it was, he agreed to give her one final chance only on the basis that she suffer some serious sanctions. She would be grounded, yes, but she should also have her phone taken off her. No access to the internet. No nothing. Cold turkey. It was the least we should expect, was his view on the subject, as proof of her commitment to treating us with respect.

'But it's *her* phone,' I began. 'So we're not in a position to do that, love. You know the rules. If it belongs to –'

'I don't care if it belongs to the Sultan of bloody Brunei!' he barked. 'It's not about whose phone it is, it's about making the gesture. About her being inconvenienced as much as she's ruddy well inconvenienced us! And if she's not prepared to do that then she's not giving an inch, is she? And I'm not having that. Sorry, Casey, but I feel strongly about this. I know she's had a bad time of it and I'm not unsympathetic, but Keeley isn't a child. She's old enough to start taking responsibility for herself, and to my mind, until she does, why should we? Don't forget how we ended up with her. Because of some pretty damned irresponsible accusations. I'm sorry but unless she can show us there is some point in her remaining under our roof, then I don't want her here. We *have* to think of Tyler.'

It was that 'Casey' that struck me, more than anything else Mike said. He almost never called me Casey; it was his 'this is something serious, take note' way of addressing me, and it meant that *he* meant every word he said.

We'd been lucky, Mike and I, when it came to differences of opinion about the children, and with our own two had managed to negotiate the teenage years largely harmoniously. Oh, we had the odd flare-up – more often than not involving Riley pushing the boundaries, rather than Kieron (for whom boundaries, which meant rules and routines, were a natural place to stop) – but once we started fostering we were trained in so many aspects of the job that, with any type of challenging teenage behaviour, there always seemed to be a clear route to hand. And, as we were specialists, trained to deal with particularly challenging children, that was perhaps even more true of us than many. And though from time to time Mike had to rein in my emotional excesses, and provide a voice of calm and reason when I'd temporarily mislaid both, we were largely singing from the same hymn sheet.

But he'd never so forcefully expressed second thoughts about keeping a child before. Yes, we'd had our wobbles with a few, occasionally serious wobbles, and there'd been one occasion when we made the tough decision not to keep a child long term because of the nature of the 'baggage' she'd brought with her. But for Mike not to see a chink of positivity in a fostering situation was a rare thing indeed. And I knew it was mostly about Keeley's age.

She was by far the oldest child we'd taken care of, and perhaps that was the nub of it. Why should we bother if she was going to throw it back in our faces? Had she been eleven, say, even twelve or so, the issues would be very different, and the possibility of 'adding value' to her impending adulthood so much greater.

But it wasn't just Mike's decision, and though I shared many of his concerns, that hug I'd shared with Keeley in the hour before dawn had decided me. If we could agree on a level of sanctions that seemed reasonable to both of us, then, if she accepted them and kept her nose clean, Keeley should be granted that final chance. I just wasn't ready to give up on her.

'But you already *know* you can't take her phone off her,' John confirmed a couple of hours later. 'Sure, if she's willing to hand it over, then fine. But if she's not, you have no right, and she knows that. And you honestly think she might? I don't. And we just can't class mobiles as luxuries any more, can we? Less and less people bother with landlines, public phone boxes are history – people need their mobiles for everything, basically, from keeping in touch to keeping a diary, to running their bank accounts – don't you? No, it's out of the question,' he said, 'and I know how much that grates, Casey, but unfortunately it is what it is. It might be slightly different had you bought her the phone and were paying the bills on it, but that's not the case. It really will be a necessity for her, particularly given her situation. What about her contact with Danny, for example? And with her foster sister? No, mobiles aren't a treat to be given and taken away as and when any more – not for us, anyway. You'll have to come up with something else, I'm afraid.'

'And that's another thing,' I said. 'Something that's been nagging me for a while now. How come the Burkes are still paying her phone bills? That's a little odd, don't you think? I mean, why would they? And it's a pretty generous tariff she's on, or so Tyler tells me. *Why?* At least if *that* were down to me, I'd have some control – keep her on a pretty basic one. But as it is, there's not even any point in us restricting the use of the wifi – Tyler says she's got enough "gig", whatever that means, to use the web any time she likes.'

'I did ask Danny about that,' John said. 'And I believe it's on a twelve-month contract with some time left to run. After that, it'll be down to Keeley herself, obviously, but till then I guess there's no benefit in them *not* paying. And probably a penalty for ending the contract prematurely. And you never know, perhaps it's a way of them saying there's no ill will between them.'

'You might be right, actually. Did I tell you they bought her a birthday present? I'm not sure I'd have, given what she put them through! But maybe you're right. Maybe it's exactly that. Which is all to the good, I suppose. But it definitely doesn't help us right now, does it? So frustrating having no leverage.'

John laughed. 'I have faith you and Mike will find a way to rein her in,' John said. Then he chuckled. 'If anyone can, you two can.'

I decided that perhaps now wasn't the time to alert John to the reality that in this case it wasn't really 'us two' at all.

In our very first training session we were warned about the importance of always displaying a united front, and how children were good at spotting any weakness in this area. Divide and conquer. Had all children imbibed that saying with their mothers' milk?

Probably. And our barricades were broken.

We didn't ask Keeley to relinquish her phone. Much as Mike had pointed out to me that we'd do exactly that with our own, he wasn't really thinking it through. He was just harking back to a time when phones weren't a necessity. I didn't point it out, though, because diplomacy is a delicate and nuanced business, but I knew he'd never part Tyler from his mobile. How could he? If I couldn't get hold of Tyler, it would be *me* that would be on pins.

As a result, such telling-off as Keeley had from us that Saturday afternoon involved only what we *could* achieve given her age and our limited status; that, bar college, she would not be allowed out for a week. That she'd go to her classes, then come home and stay put for the evening. And that really was it. If she wasn't prepared to, she knew what the alternative was.

And she didn't even seem reluctant to agree. Indeed, she seemed completely okay with it. By the time we hit Wednesday she was still toeing the line easily – simply taking to her room once dinner was over, and chatting to friends, real or virtual, on said phone. As to *whom* she was talking, and the possibility that they were paying her, I decided I'd have to take the pragmatic view – that what I didn't know couldn't hurt me. So her grounding – after all those weeks of hard-core hanging about – seemed like no kind of sanction at all. Even Mike, though he didn't say so, appeared cautiously optimistic, because it really was as if she'd read the ultimatum correctly. Either that or she had totally changed her tune.

My instinct was that it was probably a little bit of both. I think she did worry that we meant what we said, and for all her earlier 'offskies-go-it-alone' line I think the privations of the reality had begun to sink in. It was one thing to bang on about wanting your independence when you knew you weren't getting it any time soon – quite another to have your bluff called.

I had a strong hunch I knew why she was happy staying in as well. Because the old mates had melted away – had they ever been that close? – and that the terrible twosome she'd hooked up with, in Gemma and Katie, had now dropped her like a stone. Which made me almost feel sorry for her, particularly when she confessed to me that her favourite hoody – another branded item with a price tag to match – hadn't gone missing, as she'd first told me when I'd asked her about its whereabouts; she'd lent it to Gemma, apparently, and Gemma had yet to give it back. Along with a pair of expensive hair straighteners, no less.

'That's absolutely not on,' I told her. 'Do you want me to intervene? I can come into college with you tomorrow if you want me to. Or I can see about having a note passed to her foster carers?'

Keeley was appalled at the very idea, however. 'D'you have any idea what would happen if you did that? I'd be, like, *hated*. No *way* can you do that. I'll sort it.'

'But *will* you? Sounds like she's taken you for a mug, love.'

Which, to my surprise, made Keeley's chin wobble, so I was anxious not to push it. But it didn't stop me adding to the picture I was beginning to form now. Of a girl who really did have a bit of a people-pleasing problem. Yes, she had all these apparent 'friends' but, materially and emotionally, at what cost?

It sunk in then. I was beginning to get a feel for what I'd known since the day Keeley had come to us. There was a good reason why she'd smashed the photograph she had. Why it had been that one, out of the many she could have chosen. Because she hated it the most.

Because she felt so alone.

Chapter 13

We plodded on doggedly for the next couple of weeks.

Now Keeley was in college – well, busy 'reaching for success' – Danny was keen to allow inertia to take over. All the while she wasn't pressing for her big new independent life to be arranged for her, he was happy to just let things stay as they were.

'You never know,' he said, when he called me for an update on progress on the Friday morning before the autumn half-term, 'she might even make it to Christmas at this rate – which'll be the longest time she's spent in education in goodness knows how long. You should feel pretty proud, I reckon. That's some achievement.'

I told Danny that, great as that scenario might be, I didn't dare let an optimistic thought enter my head. And it wasn't like the bedevilled child had turned into an angel. Yes, Keeley was toeing the line and, for the most part, a much easier presence in the house, but that wasn't the same as her skipping home daily, full of the joys of self-discipline and education. Indeed, as the days moved on, so did her body clock appear to; she was clearly getting her head down later and later every night and, as a result, finding it harder and harder to get up in the mornings – a situation that was steadily bringing about a new problem – of her being so late that she was struggling to get ready in time for college – well, her level of ready, anyway, which involved the sort of professional make-over people bought each other for their birthdays.

'But it's hardly worth me going in, is it?' she had suggested only that morning, having suggested the same thing the previous three days running, though on those occasions without any realistic hope of success because every time I quickly countered 'I'll drive you'.

But now she pushed it, because she'd obviously worked out she had a good case to make. 'I mean it's the last day before half-term, and it's only for half a day. Only two hours, in fact. And it's only maths, isn't it? And, like, there won't be any *work* done. I mean, really, Casey? You want to drag out all that way for nothing? Didn't you say you were supposed to be going round Riley's this morning, too?'

And so on. 'No,' I said. I drove her anyway.

'So do you have plans for half-term?' Danny went on now. 'Because you know you can count on me to take her off your hands a couple of times, don't you? Well, if she'll let me. But I'm sure she will, at least once. There's a film out I know she's keen to see, and there's always shopping, of course ...'

'Like she doesn't have enough stuff! In fact, one of the things I suggested she might do to keep herself occupied next week is to see what she can try and sell on eBay.'

'Now *that's* an idea,' Danny said. 'Anyway, listen, leave it with me, okay? I'll give her a call later and see what can be done to lighten your load.'

For which I told Danny I would be very grateful. Even if a scowling stroppy teenager who couldn't get out of bed in the mornings was a universal problem and hardly the end of the world, it was definitely wearing to go through the same battle every morning, and a break from that particularly dispiriting routine would be very welcome.

But it seemed I had become ensnared in a web of my own stupid making: a web of optimistic assumptions (despite my stern words to Danny) about the reason for Keeley's about-turn about her social life. And this despite the fact that she'd been grounded for a week, yet a week later she was *still* staying in every night. Oh, we'd pondered, Mike and I, about a resumption of the phone sex – and had that been the case, we already knew that there was little we could do. But there was no evidence that she was doing anything like that. I wasn't above putting my ear to her bedroom door. Well, more accurately, I'd still do it any time I passed her closed bedroom door. And unless she was doing it via signing or semaphore, or via the medium of mime, it seemed unlikely.

Perhaps, then, she was chatting to her foster sister, Jade. Perhaps she was on social media. Perhaps she was just surfing the web. And because it suited me – suited both Mike and me – to believe that, whatever she was doing, it was better than walking the streets and/or getting drunk with so-called 'friends' in the town centre, I was happy to believe all of those. Why wouldn't I?

Which was why I probably deserved what I had coming the following morning.

It being the first Saturday of the half-term, it had that lovely start-of-the-holiday feel to it, and, having risen early, because the boys were off to watch Kieron in some terribly important football match or other, I thought I'd rise with the sun and make something special for breakfast. Pancakes, perhaps. Yes, definitely pancakes.

It was a lovely autumn morning, too, the sky a brilliant unbroken blue and the trees rising up, waving yellow, red and orange leaf-hands to greet it. The sort of day that can't help but put you in a cheerful mood. And when I unearthed a bag of frozen berries to go with the vanilla yoghurt and maple syrup, I had a big happy smile on my face. All my favourite indulgences in one breakfast feast. 'Today's a new day,' I told myself, as I got a pan out to fry some bacon. 'Anything is possible. Let's do this.'

I was still feeling jaunty, when, the bacon cooked and in the warmer and the pancake batter made, I went back upstairs to rouse the troops. Mike first. He was dressed and busy making the bed.

'I could smell the bacon,' he said, grinning. 'On my way.'

Then Tyler, who was sitting up in bed, scrolling through his phone. I kissed his forehead. 'Breakfast's almost ready, love,' I told him. 'Pancakes.'

'Totes amaze!' he answered, grinning too.

Then on to Keeley, whose door was shut. I duly knocked and entered. 'Time for breakfast, love,' I said, as I stepped into the room. 'It's –'

And then I stopped. Because Keeley wasn't in there. And this wasn't a 'got up and went out' kind of 'not there', either. Not unless she was a master at extreme stealth and forensics, at any rate. For one thing, I'd been up since forever ago. And for another, it appeared that her bed hadn't been slept in. Her pyjamas – which I'd laundered and placed on her pillow – sat there exactly as I'd left them there the previous afternoon.

Key things were missing, too, I realised, identifiable by the spaces they'd left in their wake. Her phone charger, normally snaking from the extension lead by the chest of drawers. Her enormous black make-up bag. The boots with the low heels. The tub of moisturiser that normally sat on her bedside table. The pack of cleansing wipes that wasn't on the floor at its base. The shoulder bag that normally ended each day in a flump of black suede on the rug by her bed, tassels sprawled like seaweed.

I turned around. And her giant Mary Poppins handbag, which always hung on the other side of the bedroom door. But now didn't.

And her bed hadn't been slept in. She gone to bed at – what – half nine? Quarter to ten? She'd taken water up – the glass, two-thirds full, was on the dressing table still, densely bubbled. But she'd not gone to bed. Possibly lain on the bed, but not got into bed. I thought back. Had we spoken? Yes we had. I'd gone up at eleven. Knocked and not gone in. 'Night love,' I'd called. 'Night Casey,' she'd called back.

And since then and now she'd made a bid for escape.

Chapter 14

Mike was calm personified. When he joined me in the bedroom following my exclamation of alarm, he barely inched up an eyebrow. And even when he did it was only to roll his eyes.

'You don't know that,' he said, after I'd pointed out all the evidence that Keeley must have sneaked out after we'd all gone to bed and that we had to call the police as a matter of priority. 'She could equally have disappeared early this morning.'

I looked at Mike as though he were mad. 'Are you kidding me? She can barely drag herself out of bed to get to college – much less make up her bed as perfectly as that.' I pointed. '*Much* less have the wherewithal to arrange her pyjamas *exactly* where I left them for her yesterday.'

I was talking nonsense. Keeley was capable of that much and more – wasn't it me who'd commented on her initiative? But it didn't matter anyway. She clearly wasn't trying to cover her tracks. She'd packed and left systematically, only wishing not to wake us, and knowing full well she'd be missed in the morning. 'She didn't sleep here, Mike, *fact*!' I huffed anyway.

'Ok*ay*,' Mike replied in his best calming-me-down voice. 'If that's the case, she's probably sneaked out to one of her friends' houses and stayed over. Most likely been drinking again,' he muttered. 'And too scared to come home and face the music.'

'Well, wherever she is, we need to report this right now,' I said, rattling off past Tyler who'd just appeared from his room. 'Does this mean breakfast is cancelled?' he groaned.

They both followed me down, and we reassembled in the kitchen, which was full of the mouth-watering smell of the bacon.

'Absolutely not, son,' Mike told him. 'Just slightly delayed. And listen, love,' he said, addressing me. 'Let's make a start, shall we? If you're right, and she's been gone since last night – and had planned it all so meticulously – then half an hour to fill our bellies isn't going to make any difference. Trust me, the police aren't going to be scrambling half a dozen rapid response vehicles for this one. Am I right or am I right, Ty?'

'You are *so* right,' Tyler said.

'And while we're eating it,' Mike added, passing me the jug full of pancake batter, 'we can put our heads together and make a plan.'

So it was that ten minutes later we were assembled round the kitchen table, Mike and Tyler tucking in while I nibbled on a few still half-frozen berries, my own appetite having completely disappeared as I contemplated how completely I must have missed all the signs. She'd been toeing the line because she had arrived at a long-term plan, and had clearly just been marking time while it came to fruition. But what plan? Where had she gone? Because I definitely didn't buy into Mike's idea that she'd gone AWOL just to hang out and drink.

'So, first up,' Mike said, 'is that I'm not going to be able to make the football. So maybe the first thing you should do, Ty, is to call Kieron and let him know.' He pointed his fork at me, then. 'Case, you can follow protocol. Phone EDT and the police or whatever, and as soon as I've eaten this I'll jump in the car and have a drive around.'

'If she's been on the lash with her cronies all night, it's too early for her to be out and about now, Mike,' I said. 'You won't find her on the streets at this time.'

Unless she was in some sort of dangerous situation. Which instinct couldn't help but scream at me wasn't the case.

'What else should I do?' he asked. 'Got to go through the motions. Anyway, it's what I'm supposed to do. When you report it, the police will expect that we've covered all bases, won't they? Which would include trying to find her ourselves. Anyway, we need to organise a lift for you, Tyler – or maybe I could drop you round at Kieron's while I'm out. Or –'

'No way,' Tyler said. 'I can help in this. I bet I can.'

'Tyler, no,' I said. 'Don't miss the football. That's just silly. It'll be something and nothing, like Dad says. And why should you miss out, just because –'

'But I bet I can,' he persisted. 'She was up to something last night, I know it.'

Both our heads swivelled in his direction. 'What sort of something?' Mike asked.

Tyler worked his way through a mouthful of pancake before answering. He was a strapping sixteen-year-old boy, after all, and priorities were priorities.

'She borrowed my laptop last night,' he said. 'After she'd gone to bed. Well, not to bed, obviously, but after we'd both gone up for the night. She said she had some college thing she had to get submitted before half-term which she'd forgotten about. Some assignment or other for her English module.'

'Oh, did she now ...' I said, mentally checking the box marked 'initiative' again.

'She said she didn't want to go back down and use yours while you were watching telly. And she seemed completely legit, so I let her. She even had some paperwork in her hand. But now I'm thinking she might have been up to something else, mightn't she?'

'Well, that's definitely a possibility,' Mike said.

'And there was something else,' Tyler said, obviously warming to the task now. 'When I went in to ask for it back – this must have been about half an hour later – her phone rang, and she was, like, in such a rush to go and grab it off the charger and answer it, and I'm thinking she'd been waiting for a call or something, and didn't want you to hear it ring. Anyway, I left her to it, and took the laptop, and she was all in a bit of a flap and stuff, so I'm thinking ...'

'Thinking what, Ty?' Mike said, placing his cutlery together.

'That she might not have had time to cover her tracks.' Tyler grinned. His *Crime Scene Investigation* hat was appearing above his head. In a parallel universe, he'd definitely have been a detective. 'So, you never know, I might be able to find something out.'

'What do you mean, love?' I said. 'You think you might be able to see who she's been talking to?'

He nodded. 'You never know. I can definitely try. People have no idea. There's always a trace somewhere. D'oh, Mum,' he added, 'I *do* study IT. Not that I have anything to hide myself, obviously,' he added quickly. 'But I know a trick or two. Nothing is ever completely hidden. Just ask the police.'

'Speaking of which,' Mike said, standing up. 'We need to put the plan into action. Tyler, after you've called Kieron, you can deal with the technical stuff, while Mum makes the phone calls, and meanwhile I'll head on out and have a drive round the streets. If you're sure, that is. There's no need for you to miss football if you don't want to.'

But Tyler was already rising from his own chair. 'Are you joking?' he said. 'I'm going to crack this.'

Tyler brought his own laptop down while I went through the formalities on the phone, and as Mike had predicted, because Keeley was sixteen now, the police officer I spoke to didn't seem to have that much interest. Although he obviously had to go through the motions – asking the same list of questions as last time, albeit pretty robotically. As I answered them, however (probably equally robotically), I became aware of Tyler's fingers flying ever more speedily across his keyboard and, though he half had his back to me, over at the dining table, his body language was growing obvious; it seemed as if he *had* discovered something.

He turned then and I flapped a hand at him, before wrapping it round the mouthpiece. 'Have you got something?'

He nodded. 'Think so.'

I couldn't wait to get off the phone. Unfortunately, the police officer was obviously having a slow morning, but without knowing what Tyler *had* found I didn't want to break his flow and potentially prolong things even longer – not till I knew more about it, anyway.

'Well, I think that's about everything, Mrs Watson,' the officer said, a full five minutes later. 'Now, you've made a note of the log number, yes?'

I assured him I had and repeated it back to him. Which was important – it was the number that would identify the case, if I needed to call them back and ask about progress, and would take whoever took the call straight to all the relevant information.

But it was the information we could give *them* that was of most interest to me currently. I finally banged the phone down and rushed across to where Tyler was now studying his screen carefully. 'Come on, then,' I said, pulling up a dining chair to join him. 'Don't keep me in suspense. What have you found?'

He grinned, his fingers wavering above the keyboard like a child's at a sweet counter. '*Seriously*, Mum,' he said, 'this is, like, *such* a gift. You remember what I said about her being so intent on getting to her phone before I could see it? Well, I was right. She was so fixated on getting me out of her bedroom so she could speak to whoever it was that she forgot to log out. She just minimised the screen. Well, actually, she'd already done that when I went in to ask for it back – prob'ly thinking she could send me away again, to give her another couple of minutes. But then the phone went and I'm guessing she didn't even realise she'd left this one logged in. She's got two accounts. That's the key thing, and she was on the other one, I reckon.'

'I wish I had the first clue what you're on about,' I told him. 'What d'you mean, two? Two accounts of what? Are you talking about her bank account?'

Tyler grinned. 'Facebook accounts, of course! Sorry, Mum – I'll slow down. Okay, so look.'

Tyler turned the screen towards me and took me through what he'd found step by step. 'See this?' he said. 'This is her other Facebook account. Completely different from the one she's friends with me on. See?' He pointed to a profile picture that was unmistakably Keeley. 'Same profile picture, but the account details are different.' He clicked through to another screen. 'See her age? According to this account, she's an eighteen-year-old hairdresser. You know what I reckon? I reckon she thought she'd left the other account open – you know, the one she wouldn't have been so bothered about me seeing. Must get confusing, after all, to keep having to go back and forth between accounts.'

I nodded as if I completely understood what he was talking about. I didn't, but the basics seemed clear enough: Keeley was living an online double life. I sat and nodded grimly as he then made it clear to me quite how much initiative she *had* shown.

Because her disappearance last night wasn't just premeditated recently. From what Tyler was showing me, it had been something she'd been involved in for what looked like weeks, even months. Not necessarily with a view all along to disappear under the radar, but certainly an option she'd apparently been exploring.

Because Tyler had taken me to where Keeley had been sending messages – private messages, as opposed to posting things on her wall. And many of these were to and from a twenty-one-year-old lad who apparently only lived a few miles away from us. Was he one of the friends she'd been keen to continue seeing when she came to live with us? Was he even the reason she'd ended up in our neck of the woods in the first place?

We continued to scroll through the messages together. Ty had taken us back to the point where they'd apparently first made contact, so we could read them chronologically rather than back to front. Which soon became a problem in itself, as the messages between the two were becoming more and more flirtatious – not explicit, like the phone stuff I'd stumbled upon originally, but, given the way they were going, I was fearful they soon might be.

'I don't think I need to read these,' I told him, conscious that he definitely didn't. Whatever relationship had blossomed between the two of them under our roof, this was proof positive that whatever attraction Tyler had felt for her, for Keeley he was of little romantic consequence. My hunch was that he already knew this deep down but, even so, seeing it laid bare like this couldn't have been easy.

He scrolled faster back up the list of messages, and another thing struck me – just how painstakingly she'd created her alter ego. For a start, in every photo she was plastered in make-up, with the result that she looked older than her years; an effect enhanced by the clothes she was dressed in for the photos – a selection of skimpy tops and short skirts that were presumably a part of her wardrobe which never saw the light of day around us. And, most interestingly, it looked like she was the one making most of the running, instigating the flirting, doing the chasing, building a picture of a young woman who was decidedly interested in taking things further.

She had also given herself a compelling backstory. She spoke often of her unhappiness, explaining that she was in an abusive, controlling relationship, and that it was impossible to escape from her horrible, controlling partner, since he controlled the purse strings as well as her.

'Hmm,' I said, as we scrolled through the progress of this fiction. 'I think I can see where all *this* is going.' And, sure enough, down the line came the message she'd presumably hoped for. One in which the lad – who was called Jamie – told her she was welcome to go and stay with him for a while until she got her 'head together' and that she needn't worry – he could transfer the funds she needed to get away from 'that monster' directly into her bank account.

So had the money arrived finally? Tyler had clearly read that bit too. When I looked up at him and sighed, he said, 'Exactly! It's what I thought. I bet that's who it was on the phone, Mum. That bloke telling her he'd transferred her the dosh. She could be anywhere by now, anywhere. She must have waited till the house went quiet and then sneaked out. What are we going to do now?'

Though I didn't correct him, I mentally told myself that from now on it would be an 'I' rather than a 'we'. Tyler had already delved more than far enough into the whole seedy subterfuge. And though he'd lived enough, and knew enough, not to bat an eyelid at any of it, it still made me feel as if he'd been marked by something distasteful. I was beginning to see why Mike, always paternally protective, had so little sympathy for Keeley.

As for me, I really wasn't sure how I felt now. Angry, yes. Concerned. Staggered at her audacity. But, most of all, stupid – for having failed to see what had been happening right under my nose.

'What we are going to do,' I said, 'is phone the police again.'

Then EDT, then John Fulshaw, then Danny.

Though I wondered if any of it would make any difference. She'd said she'd be 'offskies' as soon as she was able, hadn't she? Whatever happened next, in terms of tracking Keeley down, perhaps we needed to accept that that day had come.

Chapter 15

Things happened fairly quickly after my second phone call to the police and within half an hour there were two uniformed detective constables sitting in my living room, taking statements from both me and Tyler.

By now, Mike had returned – minus Keeley, of course, because she could be miles away by now – and had been as stunned as me to find out about her secret online life – which made us both pretty dense, I thought, didn't it? He was also concerned about how Tyler was dealing with it. 'The little ...' Mike had whispered to me, when Tyler was out of earshot. 'She's played him good and proper, hasn't she?'

I wasn't sure I'd put it as strongly as that, but it did make me realise that part of Mike's issue with Keeley had probably been how she'd flirted with Tyler from day one. And perhaps he'd always envisaged this day coming, even if what had happened had been a shock to us both.

Still, whatever his feelings about things, Tyler had been impressive. He'd printed screenshots of all the messages that had gone back and forth between Keeley and her virtual boyfriend, as well as some of the photographs she used. 'Just in case she's changed her appearance,' Tyler told the police officers – like a pro, 'because she doesn't really look like that normally.' He proffered his own phone, and showed them a photograph he'd taken a couple of days ago, while we'd been sitting around the tea table. 'Normally she looks like this.'

The officer duly noted the difference in Keeley's appearance. 'Well, young man,' he said, standing up, 'I think we have all we need now, thanks to you.' He held a hand out for Tyler to shake. 'Excellent job. Have you thought about a career in the police force? Because thanks to your detective work, I reckon we'll have her found and have her back with us all in no time.'

Tyler couldn't have looked more puffed up with pride.

'I hope you're right about that,' I told the officer as I saw them both out. 'I still have to explain all of this to social services – which I'm dreading, as you can imagine. I still can't believe she's done it. Let alone deceive us all this time.'

The officer was a kind man – or very well versed in keeping spirits up. 'It's not your fault,' he said immediately. 'From what we have here, she sounds like a very determined, very street-smart young lady. I think she'd have been able to hoodwink anybody if she put her mind to it, don't you? So please try not to worry too much. Sounds like she's the one calling the shots here. And, of course, we'll keep you informed every step of the way.'

I just hoped there wouldn't be too many.

* * *

I went back into the living room to find Mike and Tyler conducting a post-mortem. 'Jamie?' Tyler huffed. 'I bet that's not even his own name. And by the looks of his photo, he's *well* old!'

Older than Keeley, certainly, but given what she'd told me about the 'clients' in recent business dealings, not exceptionally so.

'Does he say his age in any of those messages?' he asked, gesturing towards Tyler's laptop.

Tyler scrolled for a bit, scanning for numbers. 'Yes! Here we are. Twenty-one. So I'm right, aren't I? Like I said, well old.'

I wasn't sure I'd consider twenty-one 'well old', but I let it lie.

'Here you go, love,' Mike said to me. He pointed. 'Only, hang on – he says his profile picture's an old one. Hang on ...' He read the message. 'No, he doesn't say he's twenty-one. She says it's a nice picture, and he says it was taken at his twenty-first birthday. So he could certainly be older, couldn't he?'

Great, I thought. 'That may not even be a picture of him,' I pointed out. 'How do we even know it is? How does *she* know it is? This guy could be anyone!'

Tyler shook his head then. 'Nah, Mum,' he said. 'I reckon he's legit.'

'How can you tell that?'

He shrugged. 'I dunno. I just can. It's Keeley who's been doing the whole "alter ego" bit here. She's basically just told him a bunch of nonsense.'

'You mean *lies*,' Mike pointed out.

'Yeah, exactly,' Tyler said. 'And look how many friends she's racked up on this profile. A right bunch of randoms. She must have been friending people in hyper-drive.'

He scrolled through a screen of mug shots of the fake Keeley's unwitting 'friends', a wall of diverse and presumably unknowing faces. Well, I thought, they called it Facebook, didn't they?

But why, exactly? Had she been in search of Jamie all along? 'Why would anyone want to spend so much time making "friends" with a bunch of strangers?' I said. 'I just don't get it.'

'It's just what she does, Mum,' Tyler explained. 'It's how she spends her time – specially lately, since she's been staying in so much. And for no reason other than she probably gets a kick out of all these blokes fancying her or something. She's a *weirdo*.'

That's the spirit, I thought. I ruffled Tyler's hair. And I was just wondering when or if to broach how he felt on the matter when, without warning, the laptop screen went black.

'Oh for f— I mean damn,' Tyler said, reaching for the charger cord at the back. He then looked across at the plug and groaned.

'What?' Mike said.

'The plug. The switch wasn't on. Well, that's that then.'

'That's what?' I said.

'We've probably lost access. It's doubt it's going to log us back in automatically. You have to check a box –'

'Well, no matter,' Mike said. 'We have what we need. And if it came to it, I'm sure the police would find a way in if they needed to. At least, I imagine so, don't you? But we can always cross that bridge when we come to it. The bottom line is that if she doesn't want to come back she won't. Anyway, speaking of weirdos,' he said, with a change in his tone. 'What's with that bag of mad costumes in the car? I nearly had forty fits when I opened it to see what it was.'

Tyler grinned. Perhaps he and Mike were adopting the pragmatic approach on purpose. Perhaps they really *were* feeling pragmatic. I wished I was. Despite the picture we'd all now painted, of this street-smart and predatory young female, I knew I wouldn't stop worrying till I knew Keeley was safe.

'They're me and Denver's morph suits,' Tyler said. 'Zombie morph suits. Good, aren't they? He's borrowed them off his cousin for us to wear on Hallowe'en.'

Which was only a couple of days away. He and Denver were taking Levi and Jackson trick or treating round the local area, while Riley, Lauren and I were doing a smaller-scale version with Marley Mae and Dee Dee, in our street. Modern Hallowe'en celebrations, eh? On the one hand, a pair of teeny, sweet-looking pumpkins, and on the other – because the boys wanted to look as gruesome as possible – a quartet of blood-spattered undead.

Tyler frowned then. 'Can we still do it, though? You know, if Keeley isn't found by then? She was planning on coming with us. Well, at least,' he added thoughtfully, 'that's what she said.'

Mike stood up and clapped Tyler on the shoulder. 'No sense worrying about that yet, mate. Anyway, I'm sure she'll be back, but if she isn't – if she is determined not to be found, which might be the case – then, yes, Hallowe'en will still happen. There's no need for you and the little ones to be missing out.'

'You reckon she won't want to be found then?' Tyler asked him, closing his laptop.

Mike shrugged. 'Who knows, son? Who knows?'

Mike was trying to ensure that life went on for all of us, I knew that. But as the weekend wore on and there was no news about Keeley, I couldn't help worry gnawing away at me.

Given the potential gravity of the situation, I'd phoned both Danny – who seemed not at all surprised by this development – and also John Fulshaw, who, knowing me as he did, and, of course, how much I'd be fretting, was at pains to reassure me we weren't to blame.

'Easy to say, but a lot harder to do,' I pointed out, after I'd listened to him saying exactly that. 'I mean I know what you're saying, but the fact still is that she set this profile thingy up *after* she moved in with us. Why did she feel the need to do that? She hadn't done it at her last carers – well, as far as anyone knows – so what was so bad about living with us that she felt she needed to do this?'

'Casey, stop it,' John said. 'For one thing, how the hell do any of us know that this was the first time she'd done it? She might have loads of Facebook profiles, mightn't she? And even if she doesn't now, how do we know she hasn't set up and deleted several of them? Given where they were with her when she came to us, I'd say that's not outside the bounds of possibility, wouldn't you? And if that's not the case, how do we know it wasn't one of her new college friends that encouraged her?'

'The college course *I* persuaded her to attend,' I pointed out.

'Casey, stop it!' John said again, more forcefully this time. 'Look, we don't know. We might never know, but one thing we *do* know is that this *isn't* your fault. So worry if you must, but stop beating yourself up. Just accept that sometimes things like this just *happen*.'

Yes, but not to *me*, was my unspoken and rather naïve response. Because, why not me? It could happen to anyone.

When you are involved in foster care – or social services, or child protection, or in any branch of the emergency services – you are exposed to a world that many try not to think about. A world of abuse and neglect and unimaginable cruelty. And what you're not aware of when you start out, you soon become all too aware of. Pretty much everyone who works with children in this kind of way will one day have it laid painfully bare.

And even before that, before the day comes when you have that personal 'this can't be happening under all our noses but in fact does' moment – you are given training, of all kinds, to prepare you for the day that happens, because you're not going to be of much use to children whose lives have been blighted if you're flapping about not being able to believe the evidence of your eyes and ears.

So it wasn't as if I was really that naïve about Keeley. I knew where she had come from, and how her childhood had been so horribly blighted, and I knew that for every kid who climbed out of their personal emotional abyss, many more went on to lead difficult and fractured adult lives. A few of them succumbed to drink, drugs and crime, and some never made adulthood at all. And though everyone did what they could for these children, the sad truth was that there were some for whom little could be done. They were already on that lonely road to nowhere.

I tried to keep positive. To detach myself, even. And when that failed, to reassure myself that what everyone said was probably true – that on some level, at least, Keeley *was* able to look after herself. And to console myself with the facts that we did know for certain – that Keeley had been the one calling the shots (whatever that meant) and that far from being groomed by some horrible character she had both wittingly progressed her relationship with the mysterious 'Jamie', and willingly taken the most recent step of taking herself off with whatever funds she'd been able to coerce him into sending her. So while what she'd found might not be entirely to her liking, she did have sufficient initiative to extricate herself from it.

'Well, yes. But only if that's what she *wants*, Mum.'

It was now Hallowe'en night, almost the end of half-term week, and Riley, who'd said this, was being a kind daughter; was giving me the gift of extreme patience, as I dissected what had happened for the umpteenth time since the weekend. Which amounted, up to now, to almost nothing. Bring sixteen was a big deal when it came to such matters. Again, something I knew, but was now becoming intensely frustrated by. But short of sneaking into the local police station and eavesdropping while her case was discussed, there was almost nothing I could do. I'd been told the previous morning that they would get in touch if they had anything to tell us, and since this was about the third time we'd had practically the same conversation, there was no way I could call them (or John or Danny – both busy with other cases) again. Not unless I had found out anything else that might be of use to them. Which I hadn't. And, again, because Keeley was a minor rather than a child now, I also had to accept that the sort of resources they'd allocate to a missing child who'd disappeared in mysterious circumstances would not, as yet anyway, have been allocated to her. Yes, they were looking for her, and doing their level best to find her – to the limits of those resources – but if she didn't want to be found, then their hands were somewhat tied, especially if she wasn't doing anything that would make her particularly visible, like wandering the streets in the small hours, under the influence of illegal substances, or dabbling in a little light petty crime.

I sighed. I knew all too well that what Riley said was true. 'And I mean,' she went on, 'how do you know she isn't curled up somewhere watching *EastEnders* at this very moment?' She rubbed her gloved hands together. It was a bitterly cold evening. 'Like anyone sensible flipping would?'

I resisted the urge to point out that Keeley had never shown any interest in watching soaps. What did I know anyway? Perhaps that was exactly what she was doing. Not traipsing round the street, shivering, with no feeling left in her toes.

'No, you're right,' I said instead, as I held open the front gate of number 57, while Lauren shepherded the girls up the path. 'I've got to stop stressing about things I can do nothing about.'

'Exactly,' said Riley as we followed them.

'Oh, don't you three just look adorable!' cooed Mrs Villiers as she opened her front door – to a pumpkin and a Disney princess-witch, as it turned out, Dee Dee having refused to don anything that didn't complement the Elsa-from-Frozen costume she'd recently inherited from Marley Mae. The only additions she'd countenanced, apart from a trowel-load of face paint and glitter, had been a couple of smears of fake blood on her cheeks.

'Trick or treat!' Marley Mae bellowed in response to this greeting, holding out the plastic pumpkin-shaped bucket she had for the purpose, and Mrs Villiers, who was a widow in her late sixties, and had seen many a trick or treater in her time, did a good job of pretending to be so frightened by my granddaughter's whoooing and gurning that she had no choice but to hand over all the sweets she possessed.

She grinned at Lauren, Riley and me over the girls' heads. 'Drawn the short straw, then,' she said, laughing as she mimed a shiver. 'Though by the look of their haul, you must be on the home straight, at least. Bet you can't wait to get back into the warm.'

'I wish we were,' Riley said with feeling.

'Well, you could always have a pit-stop and thaw out in here with a sherry,' Mrs Villiers suggested. And I was just pondering doing so, because Mrs Villiers was so nice (and often lonely, I knew) when I felt my mobile vibrate in my coat pocket.

I slipped my hand in, pulling the glove off my other hand with my teeth in order to answer it, and as soon as I saw the display – an unknown number – I just had a feeling this might be news.

'Excuse me a mo,' I said, waggling it. 'Just got to take this …'

'Is that Mrs Watson?' a male voice asked.

'Yes, it is,' I said, trying to read his tone of voice and failing.

'This is Police Constable Colin Heggarty,' he said. He could have been reading out the football scores. 'About Keeley McAlister. We've found her.'

Chapter 16

I told the officer to hold on, made my hurried excuses and, leaving Riley and Lauren to chaperone the little ones for the remaining visits, took myself and my mobile phone back down the street to our house, the better to hear what was going on.

'So did she hand herself in?' I asked him once he'd explained the gist of what had happened, which was that Keeley was now in a far-distant police station, along with her mystery man, Jamie.

He chuckled at my choice of word. 'Not so much "hand" herself in,' he said, 'as extricate herself from a less than satisfactory situation. And it was really by chance that we found her. We'd had a call to alert us to some rough sleepers in the park, and –'

'Rough sleepers? You mean she's been sleeping in a *park* all this time?'

'No, no, not as far as we know. Only last night, apparently, and to be honest, I think she was pretty pleased to see us.'

'And you arrested them? The pair of them?'

'No, nothing like that,' he said. 'We simply asked if they'd both come to the station and make statements. No charges at this point, and I doubt there are going to be any. Mr Gough was in possession of a small amount of marijuana, but we're really just crossing I's and dotting T's with this one. You know how it is, Mrs Watson. In case young Keeley has something more to say on the matter later.' As in making some kind of trumped-up allegation, I thought. A wave of irritation passed through me. She really had been leading everyone a merry dance. Except it hadn't been so merry. It had been a major cause of stress for me, and I had to repeat my mantra, 'It's the behaviour, *not* the child,' several times in my head in order to make the irritation go away. 'Anyway, the main point,' PC Heggarty was continuing as I did so, 'is what the position is now re your good selves. Are you and your husband prepared to have Keeley brought back to you? Only we're all but done here and need to know where to take her. And, from our point of view, tonight would be good.'

'Of course we are,' I told him. The words came out automatically. Though, in fact, were we? Mike might feel very differently, I knew. Though I couldn't ask him because he, Kieron and Riley's David were currently in the pub, having a 'well-earned' drink while watching some football match or other, after manfully clearing up our Hallowe'en buffet tea. 'Yes, yes, of course we are,' I said again, this time for Mike. 'Well, that's assuming she wants to *come* back, that is. Given what's happened, that's by no means a given. And what about this lad –'

'Hardly a lad,' he said. 'Mr Gough is thirty-five.'

'Thirty-*five*?' I squeaked. '*Seriously*?' I knew I sounded like Tyler. But, really? Thirty-*five*? She'd ended up sleeping rough in a park with a man in his thirties? What sort of down and out must he be? And how come? This all seemed so at odds with the profile we'd seen on Facebook that I no longer knew what to think. All I did know was that the whole débâcle had suddenly taken on a much more sinister tone.

But PC Heggarty was quick to dampen down my by now hotly fired-up imagination. 'I know what you're thinking,' he said. 'But we don't think it's been quite the sort of thing you might be imagining. As I believe you already pointed out yourself at the weekend, it's Keeley who has driven this, not the other way around. The man's vulnerable himself. I don't think I'm speaking out of turn when I tell you he has mild learning difficulties.'

'Is that so?' I said, torn now by an instinctive sympathy for the man and years of experience in dealing with challenging children, for whom such a label, in a parent, could spell so much trouble. 'Mild' didn't necessarily go hand in hand with 'benign', after all. Though it seemed this Mr Gough wasn't known to social services for anything more worrying than being a potential risk to himself. He clearly *was* vulnerable; he'd been under Adult Services at various points in his adult life – though drifting under the radar from time to time on account of his always moving around. And this time into the clutches of Keeley. It could have been so much worse, I mused. For either of them. 'And what does he have to say for himself anyway?' I asked.

'Only that his flatmate – who'd been away for a few days, hence the timing of the escapade – had returned on the Sunday night, and had refused to let her stay. Which was why they ended up in the park, by all accounts. Though neither of them seem to have been very clear on the details. I believe a local party and a certain amount of drink might have been involved.'

'And he's thirty-five,' I remembered again. 'Honestly. It beggars belief. Still, at least you've found her. That's the main thing. Though, as I say, does she even *want* to be returned to us?'

'Oh yes,' said the policeman. 'She's very clear that if you'll have her she would like to be returned. And, like I say, tonight would be good.'

'Well in that case, yes, please do bring her back to us. So, what sort of time?'

'Couple of hours, or so, I think. We've had a bit of a delay, waiting for an appropriate adult to attend the station in order to go through her statement with her, but that's all done and dusted now. It'll just be a matter of getting through the rush-hour traffic now, so around half past eight or nine, I think. Will that be okay?'

I told him it was, sidestepping the girls, who'd just returned with my brace of cold but happy granddaughters. Riley was looking at me quizzically and holding up a thumb. I stuck my own up as I wished the officer a good journey – it seemed he'd been detailed to be the one bringing Keeley home.

'So she's had enough, has she?' Riley said as she pulled

Marley Mae's gloves off. I nodded. 'Seems so,' I said. 'Cuppa? I think we could all do with a defrost.'

'Definitely,' Lauren said. Her cheeks were almost carmine against her English rose complexion. 'And while these two monkeys thaw out you can tell us all about it.'

So I did – well, as much as I knew, which was little. And with the reality so at odds with the picture we'd all painted, it seemed to throw up more questions than it had answered. Particularly in the matter of the guy being so much older than Keeley had thought and, by all accounts, not quite the meal ticket she'd imagined.

'Ha!' Riley said. 'And she thought she was the duper not the dupe. Serves her bloody well right. So now what?'

I understood how Riley felt – she was protective towards Tyler too and she was also like her father; less easily swayed than I was by her emotions. I sensed in that instant that, whatever did happen now, sympathy for Keeley was in increasingly short supply. Which didn't augur well for the immediate future.

'But bless her,' Lauren said. (We weren't biologically related, but Lauren was a bit more like me. Definitely more inclined to be receptive to the idea of second – or in this case – third chances.) 'That must have been a shock, however sure of herself she might have been. I'm sure she's going to have her tail between her legs.'

'Don't count on it,' Riley said. 'I'm sure she'll still be able to muster some attitude.'

Lauren frowned. 'Do you want us to stay here till she gets here, Casey?'

I shook my head. A posse of cross-looking women was the last thing we needed. If there wasn't any attitude when she arrived, she'd soon rustle some up. 'No, no,' I said. 'You two get off and get your little princesses to bed. I'll text Dad and make sure he gets home before she does. And I'll have to go write my log up and let everyone know in any case.' Including Tyler, of course. I didn't expect a lot of sympathy there either.

Mike was only too happy to curtail his male bonding session, as it turned out. 'Bloody Hallowe'en,' he muttered when I called him to tell him. 'Always forget about that. Place was crawling with bloody kids. Oh, and a clown. What's this thing people have with clowns on Hallowe'en night? What's that about? Poor Kieron was on pins.'

I could well imagine. Kieron had had an irrational fear of clowns since he was knee high to a sparrow. We'd never been able to go anywhere where we might accidentally see one, and the fear was almost as debilitating now. It had even become something of a comforting consolation; due to his Asperger's he'd always struggled with making and keeping friends as a child, and the sadness that he rarely got invited to parties was at least tempered – not least by him – by the one positive aspect, that he'd be a whole lot less likely to be surprised by one.

I told Mike Lauren was on her way back and she'd see Kieron at home, and while Mike made his way home I made the required phone calls – to EDT, to confirm what they'd already been told by the police, just so they could formally remove her from their own missing list. Then to Danny and John, both of whom I left voicemail messages for; bar emergencies, their working days were obviously done, and we could have a proper debrief in the morning.

I'd just disconnected from calling the latter, when my mobile rang again. It was Danny. 'It could have waited till tomorrow,' I said. 'There's nothing you need to do. I just wanted to let you know she was safe and well.'

'I know that,' he said. 'I'm just phoning you back to ask if *you're* okay. As in okay having her back with you. It's been a right pain, I know.'

'No, it's fine, Danny. Honestly. Anyway, where else is she going to go?'

'You're a saint.'

'No, I'm not.'

'Well, let's agree to differ. The point is that I'm honestly more than happy to come round. You know, for when she gets to you. Take some of the pressure off.'

'Danny, we'll be *fine*,' I said. 'The police officer said she was desperate to come back to us, and apparently very sorry, so I don't think we'll have any problems. At least, not tonight. To be honest, I imagine she'll go straight to bed. Tonight's not the time to be giving her some massive lecture anyway.'

'Well, if you're sure …' Danny said.

'I am.'

'But is there anything at all you need from me at this stage? Or should I just pop over some time tomorrow to read young madam the riot act?'

Again, I thought. Wasn't there any other kind? One that actually *worked*?

'That'll be fine,' I told him.

Mike had brought Tyler and Denver back with him – the latter to pick up all his stuff – and once he'd done so and Mike was off again to drop him back to his home that left just me and Tyler in the house. 'I tell you what, love,' I said, once I'd run through the edited highlights, 'it might be best if you make yourself scarce when they get here. I imagine she's going to be feeling pretty stupid and it might be best if she doesn't have to face everyone at once.'

He agreed immediately. 'I don't particularly want to face her either, Mum. I mean I'm not saying I'm not cool with everything because I am. I need a shower anyway. Wash all this muck off my face.'

'Oh, must you, love?' I said. 'That whole blood-spattered zombie apocalypse look really suits you. Whatever a zombie apocalypse is when it's at home. What exactly *is* a zombie apocalypse anyway?' I pulled him close for a hug, trying to read how he was feeling. Had a part of him been pleased to get Keeley out of his hair? Hard to tell.

'You don't need to answer that,' I told him. 'I'm just glad you're cool. Ever the stoic, you, eh? It's a hard pill to swallow when someone throws kindness back in your face, isn't it?'

He smelt of night air and poster paint, and his special Tyler smell. 'It wasn't exactly like that,' he said stoutly. 'She didn't mean anything. She's just, well … got issues. That's all. No biggie.'

'No biggie,' I agreed, thinking I could probably kill anyone who ever broke his heart.

PC Heggarty and his colleague, a lady in plain clothes, didn't stay. So within less than a minute of finding her standing head down on the doorstep, I was alone with Keeley, both of us sitting at the table in the kitchen, while Mike (another premeditated action? I suspected so) had gone up to shower as well. What was with all the cleanliness drive all of a sudden? But I was glad because I didn't want a row. Not tonight, anyway.

And she didn't seem to want one. She looked exhausted and anxious – far more so than she'd done on the night she'd first come to us – and seemed to have little to say.

'I'm not going to interrogate you, Keeley,' I told her. 'Just tell me why – what were you thinking of, going off with a complete stranger? I just don't understand. I mean, what did you think? That the two of you were going to sail off into the sunset and live happily ever after? Did you really think this Jamie character was some kind of knight in shining armour? Seriously, love, what did you think was going to happen? Were you just going to throw everything else in on the basis of being with a man you'd never *met*? Forget about your college course? Your independence? I just don't understand why you'd *do* that. Because the one thing I never had you down as was so incredibly naïve. I mean, think about it – how is that going to help your case for supported lodgings? If you show yourself to be so dangerously impulsive?'

The words I'd chosen – very deliberately – seemed to strike a sudden chord. She spread her hands on the table, palms down, fingers splayed. Her usually perfect nail polish was badly chipped. Then she gathered her hands up again and tented them against her temples. 'Because I thought I loved him, okay? Because I knew he loved me! He still does!' She was shouting. Not on-the-edge-of-losing-it shouting. Just as if she had to shout to make anyone understand.

I reached out to clasp her wrist, but she pulled her arm away and scowled at me. 'You don't get it. He *loves* me. He only lied about all his money and stuff so that I wouldn't dump him!' She leapt up from the chair then, and started to throw her arms about. 'And he didn't lie, okay? Never. Not once. He only told me that he was twenty-one on that photo – that photo – and that was the truth. Because he *was*. He just never said it was from a while back. That was all. It's not a *crime*. *Chrissakes*!'

She was defending him, pretty forcefully, and I wasn't sure it was for my benefit. I wondered how long she had been interrogated for earlier. Quizzed not just about her own teenage folly, but about the man who she'd gone to and what part *he'd* played. Because I didn't doubt that in the first instance they'd have been deeply suspicious. An online relationship, a sixteen-year-old girl … and a thirty-five-year-old male of no fixed abode. What other conclusion *would* they be likely to reach?

'Stop shouting please, Keeley,' I said mildly. 'And sit down.'

'I don't want to sit down,' she said, petulant. Angry.

'What's the point of telling *you* anything? How would *you* ever understand?'

'That might be right,' I said, as she decided to slump back down anyway. 'But I'm trying to, aren't I? And how about you? Can you understand just how worried we've been? How I've been lying awake worrying that something terrible might have happened to you?'

She had her head in her hands now, and her shoulders had begun shaking. 'Well, don't bother,' she muttered. 'You don't really care. It's just your *job*.' She lifted her head then. 'You have no idea. You *can't*. You think I'm stupid but that's because you have no idea about me. No idea that anyone could ever love me for *me*. But Jamie did. He still does. You don't realise. He *got* me. He was gentle and kind and they were all so bloody *horrible* ...'

But the sobs overcame her. I stood up, went round the table and put an arm around her. 'You just don't *know*,' she cried, leaning into me, as if craving the physical contact. 'You just don't realise how shitty I feel all the time. I *hate* me,' she said. 'I just don't fit in anywhere! It's like there's nothing inside me. Just this hole. This fucking *hole*.' She thumped her chest. 'You don't *understand*.'

I kissed her head. 'Then you'll have to help me, won't you?'

It was probably going to be a long night.

Chapter 17

It was a short night in the end because Keeley was exhausted. Far too exhausted to sit in the kitchen and pour her heart out. She just needed the oblivion of sleep. So I helped her upstairs, switched the lamp on and pulled the covers back, and with a tearful 'I'm so sorry for everything' between sobs, she gave me a last hug and collapsed on the bed. Might have slept in it fully clothed. Probably did.

Which left me, with the correct complement of children under our roof, to enjoy an episode of *The X Factor* that Tyler had recorded for me and which I'd yet to catch up with, and then the gift of an uninterrupted (not to mention astonishing) eight hours of sleep. The first thing I knew Mike was shaking me awake, my coffee cooling, him about to leave for work.

I'd rubbed my eyes and sat up and reached for my coffee anyway. He perched on the edge of the bed.

'What's the plan, then?' he said. 'Do we have one?'

I was glad to hear the 'we'. Apart from my telling Mike about Keeley's desolate admission, we'd purposely refrained from doing our usual debrief the previous night. Better wait, we decided, till we had a fuller picture, and some idea of what direction things were going to go now. And I don't think either of us wanted to open up a debate about whether we even wanted to be a part of that process.

I thought back to what little she *had* said the previous evening. Of the compelling nature of the way she'd described her assessment of her own worth. The visceral extent of her self-loathing. But being Keeley's apologist wasn't going to help me with Mike. She would have to win his heart back herself. If, indeed, that was what was going to happen. It may well be that she wasn't destined to be with us much longer anyway – not the way she continued to kick against the traces. Perhaps being contained in the bosom of a normal happy family was actually making it all worse.

But I had to keep faith with her if that was what she wanted right now. 'Still Plan A,' I said. 'That's the one I'm keen to stick to, if you think you can bear it.'

He looked thoughtful. 'Till the next crisis.'

'I imagine that's how it'll go, yes.'

He leaned down to plant a kiss on my head. 'Okay, you're the boss. But look, love, I know you think you had some big breakthrough last night, but don't let that completely cloud your judgement. I mean, it might be a turning point, but then again, it might not. Past experience has shown that's she's perfectly capable of manipulating things to suit herself. We both know that. So just be aware of it, okay?'

I didn't mind getting a lecture because I knew Mike was right. I was pathologically just like a terrier down a rabbit hole. Once I'd wormed my way right to the heart of an emotional warren, I locked on and wouldn't let go. But I felt sure I knew the difference between melodrama for purposes of cool manipulation and the anguished outpouring of a soul. 'I know, love,' I said, 'and I will be aware. But it's something. Let's just see how today goes.'

I threw the duvet back, and went to the window to watch Mike leave. He *was* right. Past experience should obviously make me wary. Keeley had yet to show us one single example of her actually meaning anything she'd said. Still, if I were to do my job properly, I had to give her every opportunity to do that, and if I was committed to keeping her I had to do that every time.

First, though – first and foremost – more coffee. I grabbed my dressing gown from the back of the door and slipped it on, looking forward to a half-hour of quiet contemplation before the day got properly under way.

When I entered the kitchen, however, I was not a little shocked to find Keeley standing in the kitchen, with her back to me, looking out of the front window, in much the same way as I'd been doing in the bedroom above.

'Oh!' I said. 'I didn't realise you were already up.'

'I wasn't.' She grimaced ruefully. 'Well, correction, I was, but I stayed in my bedroom. Thought I'd better keep out of Mike's way.'

Her candour made me smile. She smiled too. 'Is he really, really, really cross?'

'No, he's only really, really cross. Well, really, really cross bordering on just really cross. Manageable cross, at any rate, provided you toe the line. How about you? I thought you'd lie in till at least noon. Catch up on some of the sleep you've been missing.'

'I was wide awake at five,' she said. 'I went to bed so early, didn't I? And then I couldn't get back to sleep …' She paused and then grimaced again. 'Christ, I'm going to get hell from Danny, aren't I? Is he coming round?'

'Yes, he is. And yes, I suspect you are. But not till after lunch, so the condemned woman can at least eat a hearty breakfast. Hungry?'

'Not really,' she said. 'Not yet. Thirsty though. Would you like a cup of coffee?'

'Do bears live in the woods?' I said, as I held out my empty mug.

Keeley grinned. 'Mrs Higgins – my old social worker – she always used to say that. Except she never said *exactly* that. She said S-H-I-T.'

I smiled at her. 'Clearly doesn't have the same rule book as ours, then.'

'Er, you *could* say that,' Keeley agreed. 'She was way cool. So nice.'

'And I'm not?' I pulled a face of consternation.

She managed a giggle. 'You're all right,' she said. But she was still looking pensive about the here and the now.

'Anyway, yes to the coffee,' I rattled on. 'And then we'll sit down and you can tell me all about what happened. A problem shared and all that … Is that a deal?'

It seemed it was. With a bit of sleep under her belt, Keeley was clearly in the mood to talk now, and, with Tyler still in bed and unlikely to make an appearance any time soon, talk she did.

And for the most part she was dry-eyed and emotion-less, describing how she'd accidentally on purpose set her cap at the hapless Jamie, apparently a friend of a friend on her fake Facebook set-up – she made no bones about that whatsoever. And I was happy to skip that part as I'd seen enough of the messages to know all the details already. And this was a girl who did phone sex with strangers for money. There was nothing new or shocking for me to learn here.

It was only when she got to the part about him offering to send her money that her composure started to slip – her fingers plucking at imaginary fluff on the sleeves of her dressing gown, and her expression and tone softening.

'It was like I'd forgotten it wasn't actually me by then. You know, the version I'd made up. Does that sound really weird?'

'No, not at all,' I said. 'You'd constructed a different you and he'd responded to her, hadn't he?'

'He loved me,' she said simply. 'I'm not just saying that, honest. He really did. He said I made him laugh. He made *me* laugh ...'

'And that's important.'

'And it wasn't just some silly childish thing, it really wasn't. He *got* me.' That term again. 'I mean I know you think I'm mad and that it wasn't even the real me. But it was. It was *still* me and he was just, like, so in *tune* with me. People just don't get it that you can really know someone just from speaking to them online and phoning each other and stuff, but –'

This *was* news. 'You chatted on the phone to Jamie?'

Now she looked shocked. 'Yes, of course, I did. Loads. Well, not, like, for hours at a time, or anything. He was on a pay-as-you-go contract and he sometimes ran out of credit.'

'Yet he had the money to send you to get a train to visit him?'

I saw a flash of what looked like irritation cross her features. She would defend him to the last and perhaps that was to be admired. Well, if he was the innocent he seemed, anyway.

'It's not like that,' she said. 'He's just not organised about stuff.'

In for a penny … 'The policeman said Jamie had some mild learning difficulties,' I chanced. 'When you say he isn't organised, is that what you mean?'

A sharp glance came my way. 'He's not simple. Not in the way *they* mean,' she huffed. 'He's just got some problems, that's all. His horrible bloody flatmate, for one.'

Who wasn't in fact a flat 'mate' but the tenant named on the lease of a flat in which he'd kindly agreed to sub-let (presumably illegally) a bedroom. And who'd been away on a mini-break – hence the timing of the tryst – and who had returned on the Monday, understandably horrified to find that Jamie had a sixteen-year-old girl sleeping over. And sleeping with him? I thought about asking but thought better of it. How much difference would that make to where we were now? No. That could wait, I decided.

Whatever had or hadn't happened, it had been the flatmate who'd precipitated the move to the park. After a night in a down-at-heel (and presumably undiscriminating) B and B Keeley had persuaded him to find for them, there was nothing in the pot for a bed for another night, so they'd spent it in one of the shelters in the local park. They'd returned to the flat the next day, once the flatmate had gone to work, but at the time they were approached and questioned by the police, later that day, they were still contemplating what to do next. Jamie's next benefit money was not due till Thursday.

Love's young dream it was not.

I wondered what kind of magazines Keeley read online. Inside this cynical, embittered teen was, I suspected, a die-hard romantic. The fact that after all *that* she was still sticking so rigidly to the construct she'd created, rather than the grim reality of his being thirty-five and out of work, and of no fixed abode, said so much.

But perhaps it was me who had the learning difficulty here, because what she said next made me see it all so differently.

'You don't understand,' she said, though more in sorrow than in anger. 'I didn't care about that. He wasn't any different from how I imagined him. Yes, he was older, but other than that – honestly, Casey, you'd get it if you saw him – he was just a nice bloke. A *kind* bloke. Just so different from all the *shit* blokes I've known in my life.' She sniffed. 'And trust me, I've known fucking loads. And I'm sorry for swearing. I can't help it.'

We'd been sitting opposite each other, but now I stood up, and dragged my chair round, so I could sit close beside her and put my arm around her shoulders, thinking even as I did so that her use of the past tense in describing him was a definite positive. One which I intended to capitalise on, too.

'Love, I believe you,' I said. 'I've been your age too, you know. And in my past life I worked with lots of people like Jamie, and I don't doubt he's all the things you say he is. And if it's any consolation, he's not going to be in any trouble. They told me that for definite. But, you know, love is a big word to be using. It's a big word because it's a big, powerful thing. Which is not to minimise what you've told me about your feelings for each other, just to say that true love isn't about fluttering hearts and butterflies and sexual attraction – true love is about an emotional connection, one that builds up over time, along with mutual respect. Darling, I'm not trying to put you down, but you have so much to go through yet, and so many people to get to know. You'll probably believe you're in love many, many times over the next few years, but you know what?'

Keeley shrugged. 'What?'

But that at least meant she was listening. 'The most important person you should be learning to love right now is yourself. What you said to me last night, Keeley' – I touched my chest – 'about that hole you feel inside yourself? That's the place you need to start. That's the kind of negative thinking you have to work hard to start challenging. Easier said than done, I know, but that doesn't mean it isn't doable. Thoughts are just thoughts. They only exist in our heads. So you have to start thinking differently about yourself. You have as much right to exist on the earth as the next person, and, particularly given the terrible times you've been through, I'd say *more* right to happiness than many. If you make your first goal to accept that, then everything else will follow – then you can start building on the rest. Like looking in the mirror and seeing someone who's capable and smart and thoughtful and kind – someone who has *every bit* as much potential as the next person. You just have to find out where that potential lies, and you can only do that if you feel you're a project worth working on. Do you? Because I do or I wouldn't be sitting here telling you that, would I? But you need to, Keeley. Everything else flows from there. Including making successful relationships.'

She sat silently for a bit, hopefully digesting what I'd said to her.

'I feel so bad for him,' she said eventually. 'I know I said it wasn't like that and that they didn't understand, but I'm not stupid. I know Jamie's got a bunch of stuff going on that means it wouldn't have worked.'

Not least his age – which was more than double hers – I thought, but didn't say. 'Because you're an intelligent girl,' I said instead.

'And he never lied to me. Not once,' she said. 'I don't think he was capable of lying,' she added.

That spoke volumes to me. To wilfully play with the truth for personal gain – well, that took a certain level of intellect, didn't it? And she had enough of that to have reflected on that, too.

'He reminded me of my mum,' she said next, surprising me.

'Your mum?'

She sniffed again. 'In a way, you know? As in needing to be helped. You know – problems in his head. My mum was a bit like that. Not good at coping with stuff. Day-to-day stuff, you know? But she managed okay. D'you think he'll manage okay?'

I thought about Keeley's rose-tinted interpretation of the word 'managing'. Her mum hadn't managed anything, as far as I could see. Well, she'd managed to have five children and lose them to the care system. But it always needed remembering that heroin was at the top of the villainy food chain there.

But that wasn't what we were about here in any case. 'Well,' I said, 'he's managed well enough this far in life, hasn't he? But he's not for you. And I don't think you need me to tell you that, do you?'

She shook her head. Then she managed a wan, even slightly playful smile. 'I don't think I'm cut out for sleeping in park shelters,' she said.

I got a phone call from Danny just as I was making some bacon sandwiches for our lunch. Tyler had got up and gone off with his mates while Keeley had been showering, and since then she'd spent a little time helping me with chores. Then, because there didn't seem any single good reason not to, I said I'd join her in watching *Everybody Loves Raymond* on TV, the fact that she'd even asked me to sit and watch it with her being absolutely key.

'I'm running late,' he said. 'Sorry. You know how it goes. Too many cases and too few of us. And between you and me, certain people are being too flipping precious about which cases they will or won't take. Anyway it means it's looking like it'll be nearer two now, I'm afraid. Is that going to mess up your schedule?'

I smiled at the notion that he thought I even had one. 'No, not at all,' I said. 'And I'm sorry to hear that.' And then something struck me. Something triggered by what he'd said. The name Keeley had mentioned. A name I hadn't heard before. 'We're not going anywhere,' I finished, suddenly anxious to ring off.

I smiled across at Keeley as I'd said this, catching her yawn turn to a grimace. Despite her early start, or because of it, more likely, it was clear she was now beginning to flag.

'Oh no,' she said, 'I was going to go for a nap after he'd been. Would it be okay if I go back to bed for a bit now instead then? And you can call me when he gets here? He's only coming here to shout at me, after all.'

I didn't need to confirm that, because she already knew the drill. So I simply said of course she could. She was still evidently very short on sleep – a commodity teens needed more of than people often gave them credit for. It also gave me a chance to write up all my notes while they were fresh in my mind. And, to use Tyler's parlance, to follow up the interesting lead I'd just been gifted.

It took no longer than fifteen minutes to confirm what I thought. That the social worker assigned to Keeley before Danny hadn't been called Mrs Higgins. Which was what I'd already worked out, because I remembered that it had been Keeley herself that had called her previous social worker a bitch, hadn't she? Not cool. Not nice. Far from it. A bitch.

So when was a Mrs Higgins assigned to her, then? There was nothing in the notes about a social worker called Mrs Higgins. Just an on-duty social worker for Keeley's first few days in care. All the subsequent notes – the ones made by her social worker as opposed to those by her foster carers, panel, child and adolescent mental health services, and so on – were in the name Banks, the woman assigned to her before Danny.

Of course, it might well be that this Mrs Higgins meant nothing. She probably did. That she was just assigned to her temporarily, perhaps only very briefly. But Keeley had spoken about her warmly, which was a positive in an otherwise negative file. Except she wasn't in there. No sign of her name anywhere that I could see. Despite knowing he was busy, I called Danny back and asked him. And he hadn't heard of her either.

'But certainly I'll see what I can find out,' he promised. 'Cross the I's, dot the T's.'

'Exactly,' I said. Though my purpose was rather different. I just wanted to follow up any shred of evidence, however ancient, however random, however tenuous, however sentimental – that Keeley hadn't been entirely alone.

In the meantime, of necessity, it was business as usual, and I knew that when Danny arrived to see Keeley the riot act would duly be read.

So while he composed himself in the living room as her hard-talking social worker, I went upstairs, woke Keeley and asked her to come down. I then had to listen while he sat her down and gave her a stern lecture about how badly she'd let him down, just how close to the wind she was sailing as far as this placement went, and how she was not only extremely lucky we'd agreed to continue to keep her, but, with this latest stunt, not even deserving of our largesse.

It was the first time I'd seen Danny in this different incarnation, and I realised he was going to have a brilliant career. It's not often someone so young (not to mention young-looking) can command such respect. I could see Keeley wilting, her chin wobbling under his disappointed gaze, and in that, I also saw something positive – that he had earned her respect. Had he not, her demeanour and body language would have been so different – she would have been sullen, unresponsive, defiant.

Still, when he responded to her abject tears and saucer eyes with a sharp 'it's way too late for turning on the waterworks with me, Keeley!' I wanted to run across and hug her and tell him to leave her alone, even as I understood that it was an act for her benefit; that he was only doing what he had to.

Because if you took it back to the day she was taken into care, it couldn't help but strike me that *she* was the one who'd been let down – so badly – first by being born into a life that no child ever deserved, and then by a system that was financially so under-funded that it had little choice but to focus on the greater good; setting her needs against the needs, as perceived, of her siblings – four against one. No contest. So she'd languished alone, adrift from all of them not by accident, but by design.

Which wasn't Danny's fault, obviously. Not any one person's fault. Just a series of assumptions and predictions and discussions, all of which had conspired – even if not wilfully – to aid her progress to the place where she fell through the gap. And because no one had subsequently questioned the decision to cut her off, the reasons for the decision had become subsequently set in stone. Immutable.

I picked up the tissue box and took it across to her, and Keeley plucked a couple up under Danny's hard glare. It was scant consolation, I thought, as she scoured at her cheeks, to think her future couldn't possibly be worse. Because, the way things so often went, it could.

Chapter 18

And it was to the future, and only there, that I now resolved to look. Which was why when, a few days later, at the end of half-term week, I got an unexpected call from Danny, I had all but forgotten our recent conversation. Or, if not quite forgotten, had put out of my mind. It had been something of little consequence, after all; just my usual need to have loose threads tied up, with a fanciful bolt-on of imagining there might be something in Keeley's file that might give her self-esteem a boost – a link to her past that we could perhaps revisit without causing her more pain. After all, I knew more than one retired social worker personally who sometimes wrote to former charges, sent birthday cards even – and, oh how precious those connections were once made.

But it turned out that there was much more to it than that. 'I tracked her down,' Danny was saying, once he'd reiterated why he was calling and my brain had finally clicked into gear. 'I felt bad, to be honest,' he said. 'You know, after that chat we'd had before.'

'Why on earth?' I was shocked to hear this, having accepted his reasoning.

'Because you made a valid point. That her future had been decided – her extremely lonely future – on the basis of a statement made by a traumatised four-year-old. Anyway, suitably humbled, I bring tentatively positive news.'

I begged to differ. One of the plus points of being at the sharp end, i.e. living with a child who was in the care system, as opposed to just visiting, was that, with a fair wind and a keen ear, there were all sorts of occasions where 'right place, right time' dynamics kicked in. I'd been lucky. It was often thus. I said so. 'Anyway, what news?' I added before he could disagree with me.

'Tell you what – I'll pop round, shall I? Better to run through it in person. Well, if you can come up with a time when Keeley's otherwise engaged? I know it's half-term, but –'

'No problem,' I said, excited now. 'Leave it with me.'

So it was that the same afternoon, with Tyler out anyway, and having sneakily dispatched Keeley round to Riley's (so she could help with some firework-night kids' party she was making decorations for – totally spurious but credible) I opened the front door to a decidedly cheerful-looking twenty-something social worker, clutching a manila folder against his jacket.

'I've managed to comb through a load of old material,' he said after settling down on the sofa with a mug of tea and a plate of biscuits. From my stock of posh biscuits. I had a hunch he'd be deserving them. 'Did you notice the gap in her records?'

I shook my head. I'd not paid that much attention to the dates. I rarely did.

'Well, there is one. The small matter of an unaccounted-for couple of months. I don't suppose you would notice – not unless you were actually looking for it. As I was, of course, because I was trying to marry up this Mrs Higgins with the dates on Keeley's file.'

'So what happened in the gap?'

'Precisely my question. It wasn't long after she entered the system – a matter of days, that's all – and my first thought was that she might have left the system for a bit, obviously. Gone to a family member or something.'

Which could have been the case, because this happened reasonably regularly. Children were taken into care as emergencies and then a relative would step in, step up and offer to take them on, and, after all the necessary checks were undertaken this was sometimes what happened. A win-win situation for all concerned. And no more contact with social services, file closed.

But sometimes caring relatives bit off more than they could chew, and the children were subsequently returned to the system, creating a lose-lose situation instead. A child traumatised, then relieved at being back with known faces, then, their hopes dashed, traumatised all over again. I knew gaps in records were often because of situations like these.

But this hadn't apparently been the case with Keeley. Mrs Higgins had been assigned to her after a couple of days in care, and had been looking after her when she was moved to her intended long-term foster carer, a Mrs Stewart, where Keeley had spent the first fortnight.

'By the time the children were interviewed the other four had already been moved along,' Danny explained. Only Keeley had remained where she was.'

I nodded. We both already knew this was often the case – a troubled ten-year-old probably being harder to place.

'So at that point, the four-year-old's statement had already been made?' I asked. 'And Keeley, in her own interview, had confirmed it?'

Danny nodded. 'But there the plot thickened. Apparently Mrs Stewart had called Mrs Higgins a couple of days later, to report a disclosure Keeley had subsequently made, which cast doubt over the interpretation of the earlier things she'd said. In fact, it was Mrs Stewart's belief that Keeley had in fact meant the opposite.'

'About guarding the door for him?'

'Exactly. Apparently Keeley had been guarding the bedroom door, but to try and keep the man *out*, not in. He'd gone in anyway, and apparently she'd followed him and tried to fight him, but he'd thrown her out, and she'd fallen at the door. And there she'd stayed, sobbing, while whatever went on happened, and there she'd been found when the police arrived at the scene. Mother was apparently downstairs, tripped out.'

'So – obvious question – why has nobody seen this before?'

'Simple answer. Because Mrs Higgins, pretty old school – liked to write stuff, apparently – I know, weird – had duly entered it in her log, but, ill with flu at the time, hadn't called into the office with her report. Would have put it in an email eventually, no doubt, but events overtook her. She developed pneumonia and was hospitalised, meaning Keeley got reassigned to Mrs Banks, and then, shortly after that, moved on to the Burkes. And Mrs Stewart – who I've now spoken to – obviously thought it had, and that the decisions had been made about contact between the siblings had been made *with* the benefit of that new information. Or, more accurately, despite it. It was only after she twigged that Mrs Higgins might not have even *relayed* that information that she called the line manager to make sure it had.'

'But it hadn't.'

'It hadn't. So she reiterated what Keeley had told her. And was told that it didn't really make a lot of difference now. Though there was no evidence that Keeley had ever behaved inappropriately around her siblings, they knew she'd been sexually abused herself – she was seeing a counsellor for that by this time – and the consensus was that it was a can of worms that was better off remaining closed. The children were settling, as would Keeley, and they didn't think any good would come of raking the whole thing up all over again.'

'"They",' I said, finding myself both stunned and very angry. 'Bloody *hell*.'

'I know,' Danny said. 'But to be fair, we weren't there. And Mrs Stewart did say Keeley displayed some worrying behaviours when she had her. Said they were all very relieved when the Burkes agreed to take her on. So, on balance, perhaps nothing would have changed anyway.'

'And that's it? Deal done? Keeley isolated from them for life now?'

Danny put a chocolate biscuit in his mouth. All of it. Whole. 'Ah,' he said eventually. 'That's where the "tentative good news" bit comes in. Given everything that's happened recently, not necessarily.'

'You mean we can rescue this? Try to see if we can propose some sort of contact? Perhaps Mrs Higgins –'

He shook his head. 'Sadly gone to meet her maker. Only recently in fact. RIP. But I've spoken to my manager and he's going to look into it for me. For you. Well, for Keeley, but please don't say a word to her. It's still all theoretical at this point. And you know how these things go. Sometimes nowhere. We know the older two – Courtney and Aaron – are still with the same family, so that's good. But there are no guarantees. And it's unlikely any approaches would be made re the ones that have been adopted.'

'Fair enough,' I said. 'But the older two – oh, my God, wouldn't that be *brilliant*?' Danny's expression made me conscious that I must rein myself in. 'Sorry. I'm getting ahead of myself, aren't I?'

Danny nodded. I smiled. Again. Bears *did* live in the woods.

Chapter 19

Though Keeley knew nothing about the conversations that had been going on in her absence, unburdening herself to me seemed to mark something of a watershed, because she seemed to settle into a calmer, more productive place. Though, of course, the key might have been how Mike had changed his own perspective – he, of course, did know about what Danny had uncovered, which at least made him more sympathetic.

As for me, I had to take John Fulshaw's sage advice, and put everything on the mental back burner; leave social services to do their job without interference, while I got on with mine. There would be lots for them to do – assuming they felt as motivated to do it as I did – I hoped so – to look closely into the minutiae of Keeley's records, and see how well they could stitch together a picture that was in accord with what Danny had found out.

Only when they'd done that to their satisfaction would social services even consider taking steps to get in touch with, and therefore potentially disrupt the lives of, the carers Keeley's older siblings were with now.

And though John reminded me again that there was no question currently of any contact being sought for the younger, adopted siblings, I still hoped – though not outwardly, as I had to be poker-faced around Keeley – that the door was at least open for that to happen once the little ones had grown up.

In the meantime I was simply happy that we'd reached a new understanding and that whatever the outcome re her blood siblings turned out to be Keeley's escapade with Jamie had helped her grow.

And, a week and a bit on, I felt cautiously optimistic. It seemed the leopardess really had tried to change her spots, and though I was too long in the tooth to think one tearful heart-to-heart had unlocked the inner troubled child in her and that all would now be well, I was still optimistic enough to believe it was a step in a process; that her experience of running away to Jamie, into not-exactly-the-sunset, had taught her one thing that would hopefully get the process in motion: realising that the grass was rarely greener on the other side, and that she could, and should, try to focus on a project with better prospects – i.e. herself.

And in the short term she seemed keen to do exactly that. Relations with Tyler seemed to settle into more of a relaxed, brother–sister type arrangement, and, perhaps sensing a whiff of sympathy from him, she'd been making monumental efforts to get back into Mike's good books, too. Not obsequiously so – that wouldn't have been her style, and he'd have seen through it anyway – but just treating him with respect, and doing as she was told.

And going into college without having to be shoe-horned from her bed. Which put me in a much better mood.

'Are you mad?' she said now, from her position in the living-room doorway, and with a look of consternation in her eyes. She gestured to what I was currently manhandling, having thunked it laboriously down the stairs. 'Please don't tell me that's what I think it is,' she added.

I grinned at her and nodded. That the thing looked suspiciously like a Christmas tree was no accident. It was.

'Ta dah! Of course it is,' I said grandly as I heaved it onto the sofa to unwrap from its cocoon. 'Because today's the day. High time the Watson household got ready for Christmas.'

'Erm, wasn't it Bonfire Night, like, only two weeks ago?' she asked, shaking her head in bemusement. 'God, if anyone saw this, they'd think I was living in a loony bin!'

'Well, perhaps you are, but it's going to be a very twinkly loony bin,' I pointed out. 'Tired of fairy lights, tired of life, that's what I say.'

'Yeah, I get that, but whoever heard of putting Christmas trees up in mid-November?'

'Well, *obviously* because it feels like it's Christmas for longer,' I told her. 'And whoever wouldn't want that? Anyway, I'm guessing you won't want me to wait for you to get home before doing the big switch-on ceremony then?'

She grinned. 'Nah, you're all right. I think I can contain my excitement. Well, unless you've got Justin Bieber in to do it or something.'

'Well, Tyler will be excited,' I said, as I wrestled with the fifteen or so layers of cling film I'd encased the tree in. I got giant rolls of the stuff from the local discount home store expressly for the purpose. A top Christmas tip, but one that I supposed would be lost on Keeley. Well, for the moment. Perhaps one day, if and when she had her own family, perhaps. I so wished she had her own family right now.

'But you can suit yourself,' I added, albeit mock-huffily, as I started to pull tinsel out from the holdall Mike had also lugged down from the loft for me before going to work. Along with half a dozen bulging boxes and my number two tree. I had a busy Santa's elf-style day ahead.

But Keeley was grinning at something beyond me, and I followed her gaze just in time to see Tyler had joined her in the doorway, and was shaking his head and mouthing '*Noooo*'.

'You're Grinches, you two, so you can both just get lost,' I told them. 'Not an ounce of Christmas spirit between you. Honestly, it's enough to turn my eggnog sour, all this negative energy.'

Tyler blew me a kiss, grabbed his bag and waited for Keeley to get hers. They were going on the bus together this morning, as they would be for the next couple of days now, because Tyler and his friends were attending a few sessions at the Reach for Success centre – tasters for some of the courses that would be available for them in the next academic year.

It was quite a new initiative, but was already very popular. And, given what Tyler had told me, a successful one, too – convincing several youngsters who'd be reluctant to stay on at school to change their minds and continue their education. There was also the small matter of some of the courses being ones I'd personally helped set up, which made me feel enormously proud as well.

I also knew that, despite them both taking the mickey, they would be as thrilled to come home and see the house so transformed as anyone else would.

It was a nice feeling, and if I'd known what was scheduled for later, I'd have probably bottled it.

I spent the rest of the day indoors, with the central heating turned up to max, a free Christmas music channel on the TV that Kieron had told me about, and doing what I loved to do most – decorating. The Christmas tree, the living room, the conservatory, the kitchen – the whole house, essentially, because that was the way I liked it. Ditto stuffing my face at regular intervals with coffee and warm mini mince pies.

Not that it wasn't without its frustrations. Riley did call in at one point, but she didn't stay long, leaving as soon as she realised she might be roped in as well – literally – by a mad woman who was trying to untangle a chaotic bundle of 500 blue LED lights, whilst screaming a range of heartfelt imprecations at them.

'Why don't you just roll them up properly when you put them away, like everyone else does?' she wanted to know. And, of course, she was absolutely right. But despite my best intentions, always, it had never once actually happened. And truth be known, probably never would. I was self-aware enough to understand that, at least. 'Because I always forget to,' I huffed, thrusting them towards her. 'Here, why don't you do it then, clever clogs?'

'Er, no,' she said. 'I've just remembered I have to be somewhere, urgently, but do ring me when you're sane again, and I'll come back to have a look.'

She then deftly dodged the broken bauble I threw at her, before sweeping out imperiously. 'Jesus, the kids haven't even started rehearsals for their nativity plays yet, you mad woman!'

'Don't bring Jesus into this, please!' I huffed at her departing back.

Recalcitrant fairy lights needing total concentration, the next time I was shaken out of my decorating focus I was shocked to discover it was almost 3.00 p.m. I had been at it all day and still wasn't done. And more to the point, I hadn't even thought about what to make for tea. Let alone defrost or go and buy it.

It was Tyler, who didn't usually get back till gone four. 'How come you're home so early?' I asked him.

'Finished early,' he said, shrugging his backpack from his shoulders.

I looked past him. 'And has Keeley finished too?'

He shook his head. 'No, she's still there,' he said. 'Well, as far as I know. It's just us that finished early. I think the tutor had some meeting they had to get to or something.

So they said we could either go to the library or head home.'

No surprise that he chose the latter, then. 'Oh right,' I said, as he sank down to join me on the living-room carpet. 'Well, I've almost finished here, as you can see. Just got this holly stuff to twist up the banister and then I can switch on the lights and we're done. You want to help me clear up? Dad'll put all the boxes back in the loft for me, but if you could just help me pick up all these bits everywhere, that would be a great help.'

'And you do mean everywhere,' he said, starting to pick up stray bits of tinsel, random bauble hangers, lametta and other sundry sparkly mess.

I smiled. 'I'm like one of those TV chefs, love – it's all about the creativity. That's why I need minions to run around after me. Anyway, what kind of day did you have?'

'All right,' he said. 'But, Mum ...'

I turned to look at him. His expression was suddenly thoughtful. He obviously had something on his mind. I stopped fiddling with the lengthy pine-effect wreath that I had artfully embellished – with more, and better-behaved, fairy lights – and had been gathering up to deploy up the staircase when he'd arrived. 'What, love? You look distracted. Something up?'

Tyler sat back on his heels. 'I feel bad, Mum, but there's something I've got to tell you.'

My heart sank. What now?

'What's happened?' I said, touching his arm. 'Come on, love. Spit it out.'

'It's not about me,' he explained. 'It's Keeley.'

A new, different, Keeley-shaped cloud now descended. 'Oh, lord. What's she done now? Been at your laptop again?'

He shook his head. 'No, it's not that.' And I could tell from his worried expression that it was going to be more than that. 'It was today, it was. At lunchtime, and it was all, well –'

'Well what?'

'Well, just dodgy. I'd gone over to find her – we hadn't fixed up to meet or anything, I just went over to see if I could find her, so she could tell me the best place to go and get something to eat. The canteens there are rubbish, and her lot don't go there, so I just thought I'd go see if she was about. Anyway, she wasn't in either of the canteens and when I asked someone off her course they said I'd probably find her down by the youth centre entrance where they all go to smoke.'

'Which we know she does anyway,' I said.

He nodded. So it obviously wasn't that. 'But she wasn't there, Mum. She wasn't with them. She was outside the car park, by the road, a little way up from the entrance. Leaning into a car, talking to the man in it. An older man.'

Okay, I thought. So far, so not very good. 'So you didn't know him? I mean, could it have been one of the tutors there, maybe?'

'No, it wasn't, Mum. I mean, I don't know if it was some tutor I'd never seen before, obviously. So it could have been, except my mate Jordan was there and he came over to speak to me, and he told me it wasn't.'

'So he knew who the man was?'

Tyler shook his head again. 'No, but he's definitely nothing to do with school. He's seen her with him before, Mum. That's the thing. It's not the first time. Jordan said he and his mates have seen her meet up with him a couple of times – once she was actually in the car with him. You know, not going anywhere or anything, just chatting and that. But Jordan said he'd seen the guy passing something to her. They all think he's a dealer or something. Something dodgy, anyway. I don't know for definite but I decided not to stick around to find out. I thought it was probably better if she didn't know I'd seen her.'

'Oh, for definite,' I said. 'And she didn't? You're sure of that?'

'Pretty certain. She had her back to me. I just headed back to one of the canteens. And I thought about waiting for her, you know, so I could ask her. But it would have meant hanging around for ages. And, like, I thought it would be more helpful if *you* knew.'

My first idea, was, of course, Jamie. Could it possibly have been him? After all, though Tyler had seen his Facebook profile picture, we now knew it had been taken years ago. I asked him anyway. He shook his head. 'No, it definitely wasn't him – not unless he's changed beyond recognition. So maybe it's some other bloke she's got on the go now?'

Which had been my own second thought. Closely followed by *here we go again*. 'Okay, love,' I said. 'And you definitely did the right thing by telling me instead of confronting her. Thank you. And, look, don't you worry about this, okay? It might well be that there's some completely innocent explanation. And if not, well … Dad and I will deal with it, okay? And, look, d'you think you could do me an enormous favour? Once we're done here, get yourself changed and then run down to the fish and chip shop for me? I've been so engrossed in getting this lot together that I have absolutely nothing planned for tea.'

'Sure I will,' he said, getting up from his knees. 'Though you know, Mum, it didn't *look* innocent. She's up to something sneaky again. I just *know*.' He headed off upstairs to change and I felt a weight settling on me. I felt the same as Tyler. She was up to something sneaky again. Like him, I just knew it.

But what *was* it?

Call me an ostrich if you like, and you'd be absolutely right, because sitting amid the seasonal glow of my newly twinkling, joy-to-the-world world, my main thought was that I didn't want to know.

Chapter 20

I don't know if it was the expression on my face or just his keen nose for impending trouble but Tyler decided he'd rather make himself scarce. 'I'll still go and get tea, Mum,' he said, as he helped me fix the wreath up the staircase, 'but I'll take mine round to Den's if it's all right with you. Better that than get the stink eye from Keeley for ratting her out.'

'Don't stress,' I reassured him. 'You said she didn't see you, right? So there's no need for me to even mention you, is there? I'll just say *someone* told me. I don't have to lie. She knows I know some of the staff there, so she'll just assume it was one of them. And don't worry. We'll sort it,' I said firmly. And I meant it. Because right then I didn't know what it was we'd be having to sort. And, for all my own nose for impending trouble, no way could I have imagined what it would turn out to be.

* * *

In the immediate future, however, I had to make a decision. Tackle Keeley about it as soon as she returned from school – my first choice – or, given that she might show up before Tyler had been to the chip shop and back, and had gone round to Denver's, rein myself in (which would be difficult; I was getting angrier with her by the minute) till the coast was clear and we could have it out alone. But then Mike, too, would be getting home, at least by half past five, possibly earlier, and having him arrive cold when I was doing so – and who knew what might happen? – definitely wouldn't be ideal.

I felt a powerful urge to call John Fulshaw and solicit his advice. But it seemed pointless because I already knew what he'd say. He'd offer to come round, which I'd decline, because he really didn't need to, then he'd tell me to confront her, ask what she was up to and get some sort of answer. And not just because we needed to find out what she was up to. If there was a man in a car hanging around the local youth centre, then, in the absence of the innocent explanation I doubted would be forthcoming, it was imperative we report it to both the centre and the school headmaster without delay, because they would certainly need to investigate, and probably involve the police as well, the safety of the young people there being paramount.

So in the end I called Mike and explained what Tyler had told me and, predictably, his response was short and to the point.

'For God's *sake*!' he growled, over the noise of nearby machinery. 'I am up to here with that wretched girl and her bloody games. Another "client", no doubt?'

'Who knows? But one she's physically meeting. Which is why I keep hoping there's still a chance it's that Jamie,' I said. 'But he didn't even have a car, did he?'

'Maybe his mate's car? Was he alone?'

'Tyler didn't say. But he'd have said if there'd been another man, wouldn't he? I think I'm clutching at straws, to be honest, love. He was pretty sure it wasn't.'

'And he's probably right. *God*,' he said again, wearily. 'I mean, where do we go from here? Every time. Every *flipping* time we give her a chance to sort herself out, *every* single time she throws it back in our face. It's the deceit I can't stomach. That's the thing that really gets me. All sweetness and bloody light, and pouring her heart out, pulling at your heart-strings, and all the while she's sneaking around behind our backs doing exactly as she pleases! Does she think we came down in the last shower of rain? She's taking the mick, *royally*. Seriously, Case. I am up to here with her bloody nonsense, I really am.'

Because I felt just the same I didn't try to appease him. Indeed, his anger only served to add rocket fuel to mine. I tried hard to rationalise; we dealt in fostering challenging children, ergo we expected challenges. And I wasn't stupid – many kids who came from terrible backgrounds could earn degrees in ingratitude, lying and deceit. Often, it was the only thing they'd ever known. So Keeley getting up to mischief (if it could be called that, given she was now almost a woman) was hardly hold-the-front-page news. I suppose in truth it was myself that I was feeling most annoyed at. For allowing myself to believe her cries for help were genuine and that we meant more to her than just bed and board while she did what she liked, pretty much under our noses.

I took a deep breath. It was pointless to speculate. 'So am I,' I told my husband. 'I feel fit to burst, frankly. So I thought I'd better tell you now, in case you come home to a war zone. Speaking of which, it's gone four. She'll be home any minute.'

'I'll hurry,' he said. 'But I'll be an hour yet, at least.'

'Don't worry,' I told him. 'I'm sure I can handle it. She might have more attitude than a supermodel but that's *all* she's got.'

'And she's met her match now. Give her both barrels,' he said grimly. 'One for you and one for me.'

In the fifteen or so minutes between hanging up on Mike and hearing the front door open, I typed up a hasty report in my log. It was almost bizarre, I thought, me being perched in my pretty winter wonderland, and having to deal with such ugly thoughts. No festive switch-on tonight, then.

Instead I doused the light of the screen of the laptop, closing it as she appeared in the living-room doorway, then getting up to put it back on the table.

It was impossible to read anything in Keeley's expression. She looked the same as she'd looked when she'd left in the morning, with just the usual touches of slight end-of-day disarray.

She slipped her backpack from her shoulders, and lobbed it towards the foot of the staircase. 'Wow,' she said. 'Seriously, *wow*, Casey. It looks *amazing*.'

She then hooked some stray hairs from her ponytail back behind her ears. I watched her. Just like butter wouldn't melt.

My back was to the Christmas tree she was currently gawping at, and I felt a needle of anger pierce the calm I'd tried to instil in myself. I couldn't help it. She had completely ruined my day.

'*What*?' she said, obviously clocking my stony expression. 'What's happened?'

'That's what you are going to tell *me*, young lady,' I answered, cursing inwardly that I'd let the 'young lady' bit slip out. I knew I sounded like my mother. And I also knew that to the sixteen-year-old me those two words were like red rags to a bull.

'What?' she said again, the word coming out differently this time. An astonished-seeming 'what', which she accessorised with a nervous grin. I obviously looked as angry as I felt.

'And you can wipe that look off your face, as well,' I said. 'Keeley, I cannot begin to tell you how angry I am with you right now, so I am seriously hoping you have some sort of explanation ...'

'For *what*?' she asked, and her astonishment seemed almost genuine. But not quite. Her increasingly obvious nervousness betrayed her. I could almost see her brain whirring, trying to figure out what I might have found out.

'For what's going on. Who you've been talking to today outside college.'

'No one.' The answer was immediate.

'No one? Don't be ridiculous, Keeley. You're sixteen, not six.'

'I meant no one you *know*. And it's ...' a pause. 'Look, it's no one who matters, okay?'

She'd been about to say 'none of your business', no question. And stopped herself, just. But there was an increasingly belligerent look in her eyes.

Par for the course. And depressing proof that she *had* been up to something. 'Then it won't *matter*,' I said, 'if you tell me who it was, will it?'

'It was *no one*,' she said again, and now she couldn't help herself. 'Look, since when did I have to report back to *you* with the name of *every* person I happen to have *any* conversation with, every single moment of every single bloody *day*? Did the law change when I wasn't looking or something?'

I half expected her to finish with a 'duh?'. It was a long speech, and in saying it her cheeks had become flushed. Whoever this man was she was doing some kind of deal with him, I was now even surer of it. Surer still when she turned on the spot, stalked out of the living room and plucked up her backpack again. Had she been receiving a gift from one of her phone-sex punters maybe? It hit me then that perhaps she was covering her backside – perhaps there was something in the backpack that she didn't want me to see.

I followed her out. 'No, it didn't,' I said calmly. In the face of her own discomposure, I found I felt calmer, too. 'But this isn't about laws. This is about you lying to me, Keeley. You promised me faithfully that there would be no more of your nonsense with the phone sex. Or the fake account on Facebook. Or any of that nonsense. And now I hear you've been seen hanging around outside college, and –'

'I *haven't!*' she yelled back at me. 'God, I *told* you. I'm *not* lying. I *haven't!* Okay? God,' she finished. 'Just *leave me alone*, will you?'

Then, predictably, she stomped up the stairs.

I waited till I heard the bedroom door slam before following her up there. Again, she sounded genuine. Again, I ticked myself off for thinking so. Ever the actress, I reminded myself as I arrived on the landing, knocked on the door and immediately walked in.

She was rummaging in the backpack and glared at me furiously, eventually pulling out the charger for her phone. She plugged it in and jabbed her phone in the end, which parped at her to say it was charging. Then she faced me, hands on hips. 'Look, I *told* you,' she said again.

'You haven't told me anything, Keeley. Except to mind my own business. Which both personally and profession-ally, I am not prepared to do. You've been seen talking to a strange man, in a car, outside the youth centre. Quite apart from anything else, that's a *big* cause for concern for them. *Anyone* hanging around there is a big cause for concern. And given your past assignations, it's a big cause of concern for me too. So I want an explanation. I *need* an explanation. Because while you might think you're all grown-up and able to handle anything, you are not. *God*, how short is your memory?' I demanded, spreading my palms in exasperation. 'It's not been three weeks since the police had to haul you home from a bloody park shelter! It's –'

'I told you, it's NO ONE!'

She screamed the words at me this time, a complementary spray of spittle and all.

'For God's *sake*, Keeley,' I began again, my anger really welling. 'Do you honestly expect me to –'

And then her phone began ringing. I watched her eyes dart towards it. I could see enough to note that there wasn't a name displayed, only a number. She glanced back at me, then made a move to answer it. Or, more likely, given that she'd seen it too, to stop it ringing.

'That him, is it?' I snapped. 'Another one you've got on the go, is it? Brought you one of your presents, did he? Was that it?'

In that moment, everything she'd told me about her feelings for Jamie came back to me as hollow. A pack of nonsense all along? Perhaps that was what inspired me to do what I did. Because, without thinking, I reached out myself and swiped the phone up, charger and all. Which soon popped back out.

'Give that *back*!' Keeley yelled.

I shook my head, clasping the phone in both hands behind my back now. God knew how many rules and protocols I was breaking at this moment. But since I'd already done it, I decided to press on. Might as well be hung for a sheep as a lamb, after all.

'Give it BACK!' she yelled again, and I could tell she was considering wrestling it from me physically. But stopping short, thank goodness. At least I'd called that correctly. 'You've no right to take my mobile!' she shouted. She was right in my face now, the spit flying again. 'I can report you! Give it back right *now*, or I bloody will!'

'No!' I snapped back at her. 'No, you're not having it. You won't give me what I want, so now you can have a taste of your own medicine. I have no idea why you're behaving so ridiculously about this, but if you're going to act like a child then I'm going to treat you like one. And –'

'For fuck's sake!' she yelled. 'Christ!' Then she threw herself on the bed in apparent exasperation. I half-expected her to drum her fists against the duvet. 'It's nothing to do with you, okay? Why won't you just leave me ALONE!'

'Keeley, for heaven's sake,' I said, 'get a grip on yourself, will you? The very fact that you're behaving so hysterically about this is enough to make me –'

"Look, you're *wrong*, okay?' she shouted back, having rolled over and got up again. 'Whatever your *spies* say, they're wrong. So *unbelievably* wrong. But oh no, you just won't believe that, will you? You automatically think I've been up to something "naughty".'

Even in her fury, she still managed a couple of finger quote marks to go with this. The phone was warm in my hand. What was going on with this girl?

'All right, love?' I turned around to see Mike in the doorway.

'Oh, Christ,' Keeley said. 'Now he's going to start on me as well!'

Mike and I exchanged glances. He could see I had the mobile. 'Too right I will,' he told her. 'Screaming at Casey like that. Don't think I didn't hear you.' He turned to me again. Nodded towards the phone. 'So, exactly what's going on, then?'

'I'm still waiting,' I began, 'for some sort of explanation. And if I don't get one,' I turned back to Keeley, 'then I'll have no choice but to call Danny and –'

'Oh, for God's *sake*!' She sounded wretched. 'You have no idea, either of you! You're going to ruin everything!'

'Ruin *what*?' Mike's voice. Calm amid the shrillness.

Keeley was crying now. 'You just don't get it! I'm trying to get something on him and you're going to ruin it!'

'Get something?' Mike asked. 'Off who?'

'Get something *on* him,' I corrected. 'Ruin what? Keeley, *who*?'

'And if you muck it up now, it'll all be for nothing,' she sobbed. 'You don't know what he's like! You have no idea, either of you!'

'What *who's* like?' I was struggling to make sense of what she was saying. 'Who?'

'Christ, who d'you *think*?' she said. 'I'm trying to save my fucking sister!'

Chapter 21

It's amazing how stuck in our grooves we can become, isn't it? I'm not sure it's an age thing, because you see it in all ages. I think it's just a person thing; a by-product of being human. But there's no doubt that we sometimes see only what we expect to see, don't we? Sometimes have difficulty thinking 'outside the box', and have a tendency to fall into the same traps over and over, because we don't think imaginatively enough. What's seen also depends on who's seeing, of course. And we all bring our preconceptions with us. It's a bit like those folded pictures – Rorschach tests, I think they're called – where what you see in the symmetrical image varies depending on who you are and what you're feeling at the time.

I was still in my groove when Keeley shared her revelation. I'd only just got my head round the fact that this was apparently something about her sister. But *what* about her sister? And why did she need saving? And now I'd posed the questions, I was mentally scrabbling for answers.

They'd remained close, hadn't they? Well, with Jade being younger and presumably therefore more closely supervised, stayed in touch as far as they'd been able. And I'd purposely restrained myself from talking too much about Jade unless Keeley did first, being all too aware that, after Keeley's allegations, and the subsequent trauma, her foster parents would probably think it in Jade's best interests if the relationship was able to die a natural death.

More fool them, I thought, to think they had that much control over either girl – even though we'd been pretty foolish in that department as well. Jade could easily be involved in Keeley's entrepreneurial other life, and part of her wide circle of virtual friends.

But Jade was just fourteen, wasn't she? The thought made me doubly anxious. What on earth was Keeley about to reveal to us? She was distraught enough now to make me worry that, whatever it was, she was very anxious about it too, not to mention feeling guilty.

And then a new, even more complicating thought entered my head. Were we even talking about Jade here? As far as we knew, Keeley knew nothing of the where-abouts of her blood siblings – but could that be another massive wrong assumption on our part? Could she have tracked one or more of them down in secret? We lived in an age of global connectivity, after all. For a bright kid like her, and with enough information to go on, it wasn't outside the bounds of possibility.

Mike spoke first, echoing my thoughts. 'You mean Jade?' he said.

Keeley stopped wiping her eyes on her hoody sleeve and looked up at him. 'Of course I mean Jade!' she sniffed. 'Who else?'

I handed Mike her phone – now I had it I felt reluctant to give it back to her. All my senses were screaming that we were dealing with something serious, and now possibly also involving an under-age girl. Protocol could go hang for a moment.

Mike slipped it in his pocket. Keeley, busy blowing her nose now, using a pack of travel tissues she'd got from her backpack, was so focused on what she was doing that she didn't even seem to notice. She finished blowing her nose and sighed deeply. It was a sigh of weary acceptance – no doubt about that – but also, instinct told me, a sigh of relief. Whatever secrets she'd been keeping, they had obviously been weighing heavily.

'Right,' I said, sitting down beside her while Mike perched on the dressing-table stool. 'Now we need to hear the truth, Keeley. All of it. Come on – what's been going on? And who *is* this man you met today? Do you even know his name?'

Still she faltered. Then she looked at Mike. 'You *have* to believe me. I mean *seriously*,' she added. 'Because I swear down, I'm telling you the truth.'

'Shoot then,' said Mike. He looked like he still needed convincing. I no longer did. I could sense we had reached an important watershed. Perhaps *the* watershed; the sum total of all that had gone before.

I put my arm around Keeley to encourage her. 'I believe you,' I said. 'Come on. Who?'

'Steve,' she said.

'Steve?' we both parroted.

'Steve who?' Mike said.

Keeley looked from one to the other of us as if she'd been talking into a vacuum for the past fifteen minutes. 'Steve *Burke*? I *told* you –'

'As in your foster father?' Mike said. 'As in him? Just to be clear. As in it was him who you met today outside college?'

Keeley nodded. 'Of course,' she said. 'Who else?'

Steve Burke? What on earth would he be doing turning up at Keeley's college without us knowing about it? What on *earth* was going on? Unless …

'Why?' I said, already growing fearful of the answer.

'To give me money,' she said flatly. The line she'd been avoiding saying all along? 'He's a stinking filthy pervert and he was bringing me money. "Hush" money is what I think you call it.'

I saw anger flare again in her. I squeezed her shoulder. 'Why?'

'Same reason anyone gives someone hush money. To keep me quiet about him,' she said, 'because that's the deal we made. I keep quiet. He pays me.'

How glad was I that we weren't in my perfect festive living room right then. I imagined being in there, while the fairy lights went through their programme. First twinkling slowly, then fading, then flashing, then pulsing, then twinkling again. I imagined them providing a pretty contrast to what I knew was going to be the sort of story that would make anyone's blood run cold. I really didn't want the two things connected in my memory. This was bad. If it was true, this was very bad indeed.

Mike looked at me and then at Keeley. Looked sternly. 'You've made an allegation about Mr Burke before,' he said slowly.

She nodded and sniffed again. 'I know.'

'And then retracted it,' I said. 'Was that why?'

She nodded and sighed again. And out it all came then, in one long anguished torrent, about how he'd started trying it on with her not long after she'd gone to them, almost five *years* ago. Only in small ways at first, she said. After all, she wasn't yet eleven. Just being a bit more 'touchy-feely' than she'd expected. Which was his way of putting it, apparently, when he cuddled her. And he liked cuddling her a lot.

And, at the time, she explained, it wasn't that big of a deal for her. Used to the violence and casual cruelty of her mother's many boyfriends, and the visiting 'uncles' she'd been encouraged to be sweet to, and to charm, living in a happy family, headed by a man who was apparently the polar opposite, it wasn't like being cuddled by him even bothered her, not really – even if, instinctively, she felt uncomfortable under any man's touch. Little by little, that changed.

She didn't remember a particular day when he started trying to do more to her. Just that at some point – she was twelve by now, going on thirteen – he'd started physically avoiding her, which confused her at first, till he'd start doing stuff like offering to give her lifts to places, to meet friends, to go to the youth club, and would suggest they go for a 'little drive' on the way home.

'Nothing happened,' she said. 'He'd just, like, chat and that, wanting to know what I'd been getting up to. And sometimes he'd ask me about stuff, like, at my mum's. About the men. And saying how I was lucky to have escaped them. And he'd buy me stuff – just bits and that. Tights. I remember tights once. I wanted these patterned tights everyone else was wearing. And he got them for me, and he was, like, "Ooh, can I help you put them on?"'

I must have winced. Mike glanced across at me. 'And?' he said, his face a pallid mask of disgust.

'And I told him he could fuck off,' she said. And neither of us were about to pull her up on it.

'But you said nothing. To anyone else, I mean.' My words weren't a question.

She shook her head. Pointed out that she'd have to have been insane. She was in a family. Had a new sister – one who she'd by now grown close to. Had *someone*. Had a standard of living she'd never have even dreamed of. 'And after the shit I'd already been through, why on earth would I ruin all that? Be back in care, bounced around, all on my own again. Why *would* I?'

'Because of what he was doing to you?' Mike suggested.

Keeley shook her head. 'You still don't get it, do you?' she said, almost as if she couldn't quite believe that. 'Compared to some of the bastards my mum had coming round, and the sort of things they did to us' – her voice broke slightly – 'Steve was *nothing*.'

'Hardly nothing,' I pointed out.

229

'Casey, he *was*. He was harmless then. And he was also shit-scared of me grassing him up. *Obviously*.' I saw a spark, then, of the Keeley who'd first arrived on our doorstep. Cynical. Hard-faced. Too knowing. 'Which meant he'd buy me stuff.' She shrugged. 'You know how it goes,' she added flatly.

Mike stood up abruptly. 'I need coffee,' he said. 'I'm going to go down and put the kettle on.'

Which I knew was shorthand for not wanting to hear any more. Plus I knew *he* knew that Keeley could be more frank with only me listening. 'So when did he stop being harmless?' I asked her as Mike left the bedroom.

'That came much later,' she said.

'His abusing you?'

'No. It was never like that. I'd never let him. Not in a million years. I mean – ugh. Like I'd *ever* do something like that with someone like him.' She picked at her finger-nails in her lap. 'I'd just let him, you know, watch me doing stuff. Like painting my toenails. Stuff like that. Putting my tights on, like I told you. It was all he ever wanted anyway. Like I said, he's *such* a perve.'

'And he'd give you things to keep you sweet.'

'Yes.'

'I see.' And I did. So she was already becoming quite the young entrepreneur. And why not? She had come from a far nastier place. In her skewed adolescent mind, she held all the power. Or at least had weighed the odds and, all the while the situation was manageable, decided it was a case of 'better the devil you know'. And, depressing though it was to even consider it, she might have been right – the world wasn't exactly bristling with carers willing to take in hard-bitten fourteen- and fifteen-year-olds, was it? She'd more than likely end up in one of the few remaining children's homes, where she'd be rubbing along with kids as challenged as herself. No fairy tale. Well, unless the fairy tale was 'The Old Woman Who Lived in a Shoe'.

'But something must have changed, Keeley. Something must have *happened*, to make you decide to run away. This had been going on for years, now, by the sound of it. So why *did* you run away?'

She looked at me. 'Because I found out just how sick he really is.'

Recalibrating your assessment of a person or a situation sometimes happens slowly, with an input of mind-changing information, but other times it happens just like that. It happened now. I no longer had an iota of doubt that every word Keeley was saying to me was the truth.

The harmless Mr Burke fitted the brief with depressing accuracy. We'd been on courses, Mike and I, sat through lectures about it. As with all forms of pornography and 'deviant' sexual behaviour, little by little, he'd become habituated to the stimuli he'd had available, so, as night followed day, he would want – and need – more. And in Keeley, a girl who wasn't shocked by male sexual behaviour, he'd found someone he could so easily groom to give it.

I felt the warmth of the slim but strong body on the bed beside me. How arrogant he must have been. Either that or deluded. To think this girl – this girl who'd already been through so much – would be so malleable, so his for the taking.

I tried not to think about those early, tender encounters between them, because they sickened me most. Just as Mike couldn't stand to hear another detail, so thinking about how he had so emotionally bamboozled her made me rage to the extent that if he'd walked into the bedroom I would have leapt up and punched him in the face.

It was so shocking, what he'd done, her so innocent, so traumatised, so uniquely receptive to being shown physical affection in the black hole of the loss of her brothers and sisters.

'So what happened?' I said. And prepared to be disgusted. And was. It was Mr Burke who'd first introduced her to the commercial potential of phone sex. By having her talk dirty on her mobile to him at work. (On the bells and whistles smartphone she'd always had on contract. I couldn't help wonder: what had Mrs Burke thought about all that?)

But next up on his agenda was a visual set-up. Could he perhaps install just a tiny little camera in her bedroom?

'I told him no way,' she said. And it was a good six weeks later that she realised he had already done exactly that. 'And I *freaked*,' she said. 'I really freaked. Just to think he'd done that. That he'd been *watching* me without my knowing. Spying on me. It just …' She groped for words to try and articulate how it made her feel. 'Like I was … I don't know … like he'd taken something from me … like, my privacy … but worse than that …'

'Like he now had power over you?'

She nodded. And I think I understood. That she no longer called the shots. That she no longer had control.

'How did you find out?'

She managed a smile then. I hugged her. 'I lost a false eyelash. Would you believe it? You know, a strip of them. I was just putting them on, and I dropped them, and I was looking around under the dressing table, feeling around on the carpet, and I saw this tiny pile of powder on the top of the skirting board – you know, like, plaster dust? Like someone had drilled a hole? I knew what it was because I remember the council coming in and doing something to the electrics in our flat, and I remember them drilling and the dust they made then. And I knew what it must be before I even looked up. Because he'd said, hadn't he? And there it was. This tiny hole, with something in it. You know, a camera.'

I nodded. 'So what did you do?'

'I finished getting ready and I asked him if he'd take me round my friends – I was supposed to be going over for a sleepover. And I think he knew straight away.'

'What about Mrs Burke? Zoe? Where was she?'

'Oh, just there, like always. Watching telly. Away with the fairies, like she always is. Like she can't even see what's right under her nose.'

I wondered if a big part of Keeley's disdain for Zoe Burke was precisely because she couldn't see what was right under her nose. Because some part of her wished that she hadn't *had* that power. That, however much she'd turned it to her advantage and exploited it, subconsciously she'd wanted the burden taken away from her. Where she

233

doubted she'd be believed if she made an accusation about Burke (for me, at least provisionally, he'd lost that 'Mr'), if Zoe Burke had been the whistle-blower everything would have changed.

'So he took you,' I said.

'And I told him in the car. You know, that I'd found it. And that I'd covered it in Blu Tack. And that if he didn't get rid of it I was going to tell Danny about him. I'd really lost it with him by now. I was just so *angry*.'

'And how did he react?'

'He pulled the car over. We were *fuck* knows where, anyway by now – sorry – nowhere near where I was supposed to be going. I think I'd frightened him, you know? Anyway, he hit me. Slapped me. Bloody hard, too. And that's when I ran away. He tried to stop me but I got out and legged it down some alley, where he couldn't go in the car.' She looked up at me and another thin smile formed on her lips. 'He must have been *shitting* it.'

I removed my arm from round her shoulder so I could give my arm a stretch. 'And then you went to the police, made the allegation – almost as an afterthought, according to the officers who found you – then ended up at ours. Why didn't you tell them all of this?'

'Because by the time they picked me up I'd thought it through a bit. I decided if I could just get away from him that would be okay. I knew I was old enough to look after myself and I just thought they could put me up somewhere till I was old enough to go into supported lodgings – I'd already been talking about all that with Danny anyway. But they were having none of it. As far as they were concerned there was nowhere else for me to go, and they were going to take me back there, no arguments. And you *can't* argue when you're not sixteen.' This I knew to be true. 'And it hit me that the only way I could stop them taking me back there would be to tell them he'd tried to touch me up. So that's what I did. And bingo. They brought me here.'

I acknowledged this with my own smile. 'Indeed they did,' I said. 'But then you changed your mind and retracted it. Why on earth did you do that?'

Again that look of surprise that I hadn't grasped the obvious. 'Because it was a complete waste of time, wasn't it? You saw – no one believed me. I *knew* no one would believe me. Yes, it got me out of there, but you have no idea how good he is. Everyone loves him. Everyone thinks he's such a *hero*. And he's right, isn't he?'

'He is?'

'In what he told me. That everyone knew about my background, how I'd done stuff with Mum's boyfriends. How I'd come out of this shithole and was always flirting with him and everything, and how I was being malicious because he wouldn't give in to me – you know, let me do what I liked, usual teenage stuff and so on. And how kids from places like where I'd come from were always making allegations about their carers just to make trouble.'

It happened. I knew that. It happened depressingly often. You could never be complacent. I remembered all the seminars.

'And he said he'd cut my phone off. And I wouldn't have any money. And he said if I told them I'd lied to them about him, I could still have both. And I *needed* both, didn't I? So I did.'

I wasn't about to query Keeley's notion of 'need'. Who was I to do that? Her perception of what she needed to survive had been forged in a foundry I'd thankfully never entered. 'So now,' I said, fearing hearing what I feared to be true. 'You've been meeting up with him –'

'I've always been in touch with him, Casey. All along.'

'But physically meeting him – that's new.'

She nodded. 'I had to.'

'Why?'

'Because he's started on Jade. On *his own daughter*!'

'You know this for a fact?'

She looked appalled. 'You think she'd *joke* about something like that?'

'I'm sorry,' I said, putting my arms around her again. 'So she's told you.'

'I mean, can you even *believe* that? I mean, yeah, with me, I get it. I'm like nothing to do with him, am I? But, God, she's his *kid*!'

Adopted kid, obviously. But I was no more inclined to make that distinction than Jade was. She was right to be appalled.

As if the word 'appalled' even came near.

Chapter 22

It was the strangest thing. We'd been an hour and a half sitting up in Keeley's bedroom, and it had long since become dark, and when I came downstairs, leaving Keeley to get changed into her joggers and wash her face, it was as if I was stepping into another world. Just coming down the fairy-light-flanked stairs, into the warm glow of our Christmas living room, it was as if I was seeing the result of the day's labours properly for the first time. And it looked so otherworldly, so at odds with the world that lay outside the front door, almost as if it hadn't even been me who'd done it – as if the work had been done by an army of tiny elves.

The magic was shattered by an explosive grunt, which seemed to come out of nowhere – there were no lights on, just the ones on the tree – but soon revealed itself to be Mike, who started as if stung, woken up by the volume of his own snoring.

I switched on the main light, and he came fully awake – he'd been flat out on the sofa, presumably shattered after his day at work – and the tang of vinegar led my nose to where his empty plate sat on the coffee table, and I felt a rush of emotion; simple gratitude for the uncomplicated life we led.

Well, largely uncomplicated. In a professional capacity, it was often anything but. And right now, it was as far from 'uncomplicated' as it was possible for it to be. I could already see the ripples heading outwards from where the stone had hit the water. So many lives would be changed beyond recognition by this.

Mike sat up. I went and joined him, perching on the edge of the sofa.

'So?' he said.

'Uurgh,' I said, putting my face in my hands momentarily. 'It's pretty bad, love,' I said, as I rolled my stiff shoulders – as much as anything else, I knew I'd pay for the decorating bonanza tomorrow. A tomorrow which looked like being a very different kind of tomorrow than I'd imagined a couple of hours ago. And then some.

I ran by the rest of what Keeley had told me with Mike, and by the time she came down we were in the kitchen making coffee, and a plan for what we needed to do next. Given Keeley's disclosures about what might be happening with Jade, it was imperative we act right away.

Keeley accepted a coffee and we regrouped round the kitchen table. 'So,' Mike said, 'what we need to know from you, love, is what happened today. What was your plan when you met him outside school?'

She nodded towards the phone. 'I was going to try and record him. Get something on there that would incriminate him. Otherwise he'd only deny it, I know he would. He still will. That's why I didn't want you to know anything about it till I'd got some evidence.'

'What, of him confessing to you?' I asked. 'You really expected him to do that?'

Keeley shook her head. Then she began looking sheepish as she described what her plan had actually been. I don't know if she'd been watching one too many episodes of *Crime Scene Investigation* with Tyler, but she'd certainly given the matter a lot of thought, and had decided that her best bet would be to trap him into admitting to what he'd been up to.

'Do you even *know* what he's been up to?' Mike asked reasonably enough. 'I mean, for sure?'

'No. That's the thing. Not what he's been up to since I've been gone, obviously – not that he couldn't easily wriggle out of,' Keeley admitted. 'And Jade's not actually found anything that would incriminate him. He's too clever for that.'

'So what makes you so sure he's behaving inappropriately with her?' Mike asked.

'Because of what she said. About a week back. About how he'd been weirding her out. I mean, he's always weirded her out a bit, to be honest. But last week she said she came home from school early and he was in her bedroom. I mean, like, *weirdly* in her bedroom. Like when he shouldn't have even been at home.'

'What about her mum. What about Zoe?'

'Out shopping. And he hadn't heard her come in, and didn't expect her, either. And she was telling me this –

thinking he was going through her drawers to find her diary or something – and, of course, I knew straight away that he probably *wasn't* doing that. And then she told me he was on his hands and knees fiddling about with something near one of her plug sockets, and that he made some lame excuse, and I was, like, oh *God*, because I knew what he was probably *really* up to. And that's when I decided I had to do something.'

My mind was reeling now. The picture she'd painted was so compelling. It was one of the most horrifying stories I think I'd ever heard. Horrifying in itself, but what made it doubly terrible was that this man was a foster carer, and not only that, he was an adoptive father as well.

Which meant he'd have had to go through the same rigorous background checks Mike and I had – and probably even more so. Just as a foster carer he'd have had to go before a panel, and as a prospective adoptive father, which he'd been first, of course, that process would have been repeated more than once. The adoption process was long, slow and rigorous for good reason; to ensure things like this didn't, couldn't, happen. No system was foolproof, of course, and people changed, obviously, but it sent a chill through me to think that it looked like it *had* happened, and to consider the possibility that the adopting and subsequent fostering of two girls had been part of some sick plan all along. I could only pray that actually acting on his impulses had been something that hadn't happened till much, much later – that only Keeley had suffered at his hands.

I'd not eaten, and perhaps should, because I felt suddenly nauseous.

'Does Jade know what you've been doing?' I asked.

Keeley shook her head. 'I mean she knows how I feel about him, obviously, and I agreed that what she'd told me sounded pretty creepy. She obviously doesn't know I speak to him and get money off him and all that. I'd never have told her that. Oh, and that was another thing. She'd had a mate round and he was, like, all over both of them, saying why didn't her friend come for a sleep-over some time, that kind of thing. And *that* weirded Jade out as well.

'So I had to *do* something. And I knew there'd be no point in telling Danny. Not yet. Or you. Not after saying what I said before and then retracting it and everything. Not till I could actually prove it.' She nodded towards the phone again. 'So that's what I tried to do. That's what we *still* have to do.'

'By doing what?' Mike asked.

'By using my initiative.' Keeley glanced at me as she said this. 'I knew there was no point in saying anything about Jade, because he'd freak. So – this was by phone, right – I told him' – she lowered her gaze now – 'that I was saving up to buy an iPad for college, and that if he wanted to help out I didn't mind if he wanted to do some … er … stuff.'

She was reddening. Which I found strangely touching. It felt like an acceptance that the life she'd been living, that the things she'd been doing, had some moral question mark hanging over them after all.

I was also aware of Mike wincing out of the corner of my eye. 'Okay,' I said, 'the thinking being that you could lure him into saying something that would incriminate him. But surely he wouldn't be so stupid – and surely the evidence of the texts would be enough?'

Keeley shook her head. 'No, no texts. He isn't that stupid. This was a call. I just wanted to get him to come and meet me. Actually, he *is* that stupid. He's that much of a perve that he actually did. I tried last week. We went for a drive – in my lunch hour, don't worry,' she added. 'But it didn't work. I managed to get the mic on. But the sound was completely muffled by my jumper. And I would have tried again today, only there were a couple of the staff hanging around out the front. And you could tell they had their eye on him.' She glanced at me. 'I suppose it was them who told you I'd been speaking to him?'

I allowed myself a nod. It was all going to be academic now, anyway. 'But you've been texting, you and Jade?' Mike said, picking up her barely charged phone. 'Here,' he said, handing it to her. 'You might want to plug it in.'

Keeley stood up and did so. And as she turned back to come and sit back at the table, I could see that it was as if a weight had been lifted from her. No tears now. Just grim determination.

'You need to eat,' I said. 'How do elderly fish and chips sound? And while you do that, I have some phone calls to make.'

'I could just about manage a fish sandwich,' Keeley said. 'If that's okay?' She smiled a weary smile.

Mike stood up. 'I'll do that,' he said, nodding towards me. 'While Keeley makes us all more coffee. Love, you get the short straw, I'm afraid.'

* * *

There have been occasions in my lifetime when I have cried, really cried, over one thing or another – the death of my grandmother being the one that sticks in my mind most vividly. I remember feeling such overwhelming exhaustion afterwards. As if I'd run a marathon rather than just sat down and wept. Discombobulated. Drained. Slightly light headed.

I hadn't cried over this. I didn't think I would – I was too angry. But watching Keeley rise from the table then, to make the coffee, while Mike organised some tea for her, I saw what looked like that same kind of emotional exhaustion. As if she was waiting for her fate to be delivered along with the fish. It made her seem her age, finally. Perhaps younger.

I shut myself off in the living room, as instructed, and called Tyler. I explained as much as I could explain without freaking him out, and asked how he felt about sleeping over at Denver's and going to school from there in the morning. I knew Denver's mum wouldn't mind. 'I'll get Dad to drop round whatever you need,' I added, 'but it'll be about an hour before he'll be able to get to you. Is that okay? I have a few more calls to make, and I obviously want Dad to stay with Keeley while I make them.'

Tyler assured me that would be fine – that it suited him better, really. 'I'd only be up in my room, wouldn't I?' he pointed out. 'While the coppers are round.'

'You're a sweetheart,' I told him.

'Just being sensible,' he assured me. 'God, Mum, I feel *dead* sorry for her.'

And perhaps a more appropriate order had been re-established in their relationship, I suspected. Which was fine, and completely as it should be.

The next call I had to make – and definitely the most difficult – was to John Fulshaw. I wouldn't be leaving a message on his work answerphone, either. He had long ago made it clear that, in absolute emergencies, I could call him on his mobile or his home phone, at any time of day or night. I'd rarely, thank goodness, had to do so up to now, EDT being the go-to people in most fostering-related after-hours crises. But this was new territory and I knew I should do nothing without his guidance; it wasn't just Keeley that was involved here – a whole family looked like being torn apart.

He answered after three rings, and, perhaps already knowing this must be serious, his answering 'Casey, to what do I owe the pleasure?' was already tinged with irony. Pleasure it would definitely not be. I broke the news to him as dispassionately as I could.

'Jesus Christ!' he finally exclaimed after listening for a long time in silence. 'And you're absolutely sure all of this is true? I'm sorry to have to ask, because I know you wouldn't have called me if you doubted it, but, well, after the last time … And she's proven herself to be quite the little actress, hasn't she?'

I agreed that she had, but that I didn't doubt the veracity of her claims a single bit. 'Seriously, John,' I finished, 'how I wish there *were* some doubt. But yes, I'm absolutely convinced she's told us the truth. Everything about it completely stacks up. The only trouble is that she has no concrete evidence. Hence her being in such a state about it all. She feels terrible, of course – responsible for putting Jade at risk – because if she hadn't retracted her last statement we wouldn't be in this situation, would we?'

'I'm not sure that's true,' John said. 'No one ever took her initial allegations seriously, anyway. No, if this is true – and I trust your instincts on this, Casey – it's us who are the guilty ones. All of us, collectively, as a service. For only seeing what we want to. For being too focused on the potential risks fostered children can visit on their carers, and not nearly enough on the possibility that it might be the other way around. Right, then,' he went on, with an edge in his voice, 'you all need to sit tight there for a little bit longer, while I do what I have to do. But please assure Keeley that she won't be in any trouble, won't you? I'll try to get back to you within the hour.'

'Okay,' I said, 'I will. Anything else I can tell her? Will she have to tell all of this to someone else? Make a formal statement? What's going to happen now, anyway? I have this vision of a patrol car speeding to the Burkes' to take Jade to a place of safety, but that's not quite how it's going to happen, surely?'

'It well might, more or less,' he said, 'though that'll depend on a number of factors, not least on whatever conversation is had with Jade herself. And I have no idea what might happen to Burke – to the Burkes, even – much less when. But yes, in the here and now, Keeley will undoubtedly need to make a statement to the police – who I'll be ringing now – and no doubt Danny will need to take some sort of statement from her too. I'll call him once I've spoken to the police, save you having to go through it all a second time. Doubtless he'll ring you too, but, as I say, in the meantime sit tight and keep Keeley close. Oh, and for obvious reasons, keep her phone close as well. There could be crucial evidence on there, couldn't there? Text trails and calls and so on … oh, and specially if money's changed hands via her banking app.' He laughed then, surprising me. 'Hark at me. As if I even know what I'm talking about. Anyway, here we go again, eh?'

Yes, here we go again, I thought. But not to the same place we'd been to the last time, with a hapless young man more the victim than the perp. No, this time to a place where there be monsters.

Chapter 23

It was like we were standing at the top of a snowy hill, and had just set a snowball in motion. It was a familiar metaphor. Often used, but, as we sat sipping coffee and grazing on the tin of Quality Street I'd decided to open early, it struck me that this was exactly what the immediate future might be like, as what we'd formed into a ball and started rolling down that hill began to pick up everything in its path.

Most of this, of course, would involve the Burkes. It was pointless to speculate about what Zoe Burke might or might not know about her husband's secret habit – down the decades there'd been cases of both complete ignorance, on the one hand, and full-on duplicity on the other, plus every shade of grey in between.

What I did know, having seen the fall-out from countless undesirable domestic set-ups – inescapably, in the form of the many kids we'd fostered – was that certain evils often went hand in hand with a fearsomely good talent for deception. If Steve Burke had kept his grisly secret from all the agencies who'd grilled him, assessed him and re-assessed him down the years, it was perfectly possible that he could have kept it from his wife. Not only that – while I knew I had to keep an open mind, I just couldn't get my head round the idea that an adoptive and foster mother would allow such abominations to go on under her roof, even if all she had was the tiniest hunch that it might be.

It made me look at Keeley's disdain for her in a different light too. Just as the children of divorce often transferred the blame onto the partner who'd been left, rather than the leaver, perhaps Keeley's lack of respect for her foster mother was, at least in part, down to being so exasperated by her failure to see what was going on right under her nose.

But none of this was for me to do more with than ponder. It would all, as the saying goes, come out in the wash, and, like dirty washing has done for centuries, no doubt be aired all over the tabloid press, too.

'Do you think Steve will be arrested?' Keeley asked over the chatter on the television. None of us were really watching it. Just staring at it, reluctant to turn it off. It was a distraction, at least, from our thoughts.

The skin on Mike's face was stretched tight across his jaw. As a man, having to contemplate men's basest natures, he didn't take this kind of thing well. 'I should bloody hope so,' he said. He glanced down at his watch. 'I wouldn't be surprised if the police aren't round there even as we speak.'

I glanced at Keeley. She looked serious, but also reso-lute. 'I hope they are,' she said. 'I should have told the

truth a long time ago. He deserves everything he gets.'
She had her mug clasped in both hands, and her glittery
nail polish was catching the light as she talked. Her chin
lifted slightly. 'And I don't care if he tells them about me
taking stuff off him, either. I don't care if I get in trouble
for that. What's the worst they can do?'

'You won't, love,' I promised her, hoping I was right.
But I must be, surely? There was no crime in taking money
and gifts from your former foster parent, as far as I knew.
Well, as long as you declared it on your tax return, anyway.
And since Keeley wasn't at work yet, that didn't apply.
She'd be well under the tax threshold for a good while yet,
wouldn't she?

I almost laughed out loud at the ridiculous nature of my
thinking. 'He was the one doing wrong here, love,' I told
her. 'And whatever part you played, even though you're
sixteen now, you're still the minor and he is the so-called
responsible adult.'

'Neither of which terms comes even *close* to the things
I'd be calling him,' Mike said with feeling, 'if we didn't
have rules about swearing in this house!'

Which made Keeley giggle. But it wasn't long
before we returned to our default position, of sitting
glumly, as if trapped in a particularly slow doctor's waiting
room, all of us talked out – particularly me and Keeley –
pretending to watch the TV but mostly immersed in our
thoughts.

But barely forty minutes had passed before the house
phone began trilling, and both Mike and Keeley looked to
me to pick it up.

It was John again. 'Casey, the police should be with you within the next fifteen minutes. Not the officers who dealt with her before, which is a pity, but there you go. One thing we can't control is other people's shifts. Anyway, that's the next step.'

'For Keeley to make a formal statement to them, right? And she can do that here?'

'Yes, absolutely,' John said. 'And as her primary carer you'll be needed to make a statement too.'

'And Jade? What's going to happen there? Does it all have to wait until they've been to us?'

'Oh, not at all,' John reassured me. 'As far as I'm aware, Stephen Burke is being taken down for questioning as we speak. And Jade will also be removed – social services are obviously attending – and taken to a place of safety while the investigation gets under way.'

In another scenario, I reflected, taken to a foster home just like ours; a call to the emergency duty team, a series of conversations as they went down their list and, should they end up at W for Watson, it could well have been us. I wondered if Helena Curry was on duty.

'What about Zoe Burke?' I asked him.

'No idea as yet,' he said. 'Much will obviously depend on what, if anything, she knew. I imagine she'll be asked to make a statement too.'

I tried to put myself in Zoe Burke's shoes and found I couldn't. Assuming she knew nothing, this would hit her like a ton of bricks. Or, using my analogy, like she'd been hit by that fast-moving snowball – subsumed by it, rolled into the greater mass of debris and, at some point – a point a fair way down the line, I imagined – released as it melted and plopped back into her life, to find it irrevocably changed.

'And if she knew nothing?' I asked John, feeling a stab of female solidarity, 'will they just accept that and put Jade back with her again?'

Having heard Jade being mentioned, Keeley had come across and joined me, and was now mouthing stuff at me – 'Where is she? Is she okay? Will I be able to speak to her?' I hushed her with my hand as John explained that he couldn't answer that question – nobody could until the investigation into Keeley's allegations got under way, and there was no way anyone would even guess at the bigger picture. 'What about contact?' I asked him. 'Contact with Keeley, I mean.'

Again, he told me that would probably be a no-go for the moment, it being unlikely that any legal team would allow the girls to communicate for the moment, and though I was at pains not to convey that to Keeley just yet, she wasn't stupid; she could tell by my expression and 'oh, I see's', and even as I put down the phone she'd started crying. 'So that's another sister I've managed to lose!' she said. 'For fuck's *sake!*'

I took her in my arms and held her tight. 'In the *short* term, okay? Just for the moment, that's all.' I then held her away from me. 'Come on. Buck up, sweetheart. The police will be here soon. This is *about* your sister, isn't it? You're doing the right thing. Doing a *good* thing. You are not going to lose her, okay? If anything, you'll probably be closer.'

Mike was hovering with the tissue box by now, bless him. I plucked one out and handed it to Keeley, hoping I was at least on sure ground about that. And if it turned out I wasn't, I'd bloody fight for it. 'Come on, dry your eyes,' I told her. 'And try to get your head straight. You've got a lot of talking to do again. You'll need to tell them exactly what you told me. Everything. Warts and all. I know it's going to be long and stressful, but don't hold anything back. Think you can do that?'

Keeley produced a wry and thoughtful smile. 'Be easier this time,' she said, dabbing at the skin under her eyes. 'It's not exactly hard, is it, telling the truth? Much easier than when you're having to tell lies.'

I gave her another hug. 'Exactly,' I agreed. 'And a good lesson to learn. And we're both here to support you. So there's nothing to be frightened of, okay?'

And, as if by design, there was a knock at the door. Policemen hardly ever seemed to ring the bell. Why was that?

'I'll let them in,' Mike said, 'then I'll get Ty's uniform and bag for him.' He leaned to peck me on the cheek. 'And I won't hurry back, if it's all the same to you.'

Which it was. I knew he didn't want to have to hear it all again.

I didn't either. But I found myself strangely energised. Not excited – you could never be excited about such a thing – but energised by the realisation that we'd reached a very important watershed. A place from which Keeley might emerge with her past partly purged, freeing her up to actually feel she had a future.

* * *

The police officers, one male and, thankfully, one female, introduced themselves to Keeley only by their first names. They were both quite young – another plus – and visibly heartened to find themselves conducting business in my living room, as if playing police officers in a Christmas movie (albeit an early one). *Tired of Christmas, tired of life* – the mantra came to me unbidden. I was glad to see these two officers – Dean and Laura – were not yet irreversibly hard-bitten and cynical.

They both said they'd have tea, and by the time I'd returned with a pot and some more warm mince pies Keeley was already deep into her story. She was explaining how she'd happily taken cash and gifts from Burke – not for phone sex in his case, there was no need for that now – but simply to ensure her continued silence.

'I know that's wrong,' she said. 'And I feel really ashamed of myself now. I mean, I know it was only me involved, and at first' – she glanced up at me – 'I didn't see how it was anyone else's business. It wasn't like I was asking or anything, he was just, like, throwing it at me. But then I met this lad' – I noticed the voice recorder now in place on the coffee table – 'and, like, it really made me think about what I was doing with my life.' She looked at the officers in turn. 'You know about that, right?' They nodded. 'Anyway, I, like, ran away to be with him.' She looked at me apologetically. 'And he was so nice. So nice *to* me – so genuinely, properly nice, and it just made me hate myself. And made me hate that pervert even more. Because it was *him* who made me what I'd become.' She paused to pick up the glass of orange juice I'd brought her.

I reflected again. She was such a bright girl. Which made me even more furious, because her education had been messed up as well. All those ripples of destruction flowing out.

'Jamie, his name was,' Keeley went on. 'And I told him. Not lots. Just a bit about the things Steve had had me do. Only little bits, mind, and he was, like, *so* disgusted, it really hit me just how fucked – sorry – messed up it all was. So I would have told anyways. I knew I would.'

I took up position in the armchair across from the tree. This part was all news to me. I'd had no idea she'd told Jamie anything about her *real* life. I had imagined it all to have been somewhat superficial, especially since she'd told me that she'd found herself almost inhabiting the version of herself she'd created for him. Well, well.

Despite the voice recorder, Dean was scribbling furiously in his book, while Laura continued to gently probe Keeley about some point or another. Then, finally, she addressed me. 'I think we have all we need for now, Mrs Watson. As I've just explained to Keeley, Mr Burke has been arrested and will be questioned. I just need to arrange a time for the two of you to come down to the station, to sign an official statement, which will obviously be recorded. Will some time tomorrow suit you both?' She glanced at Keeley again. 'I know it's a pain, sweetheart, but that will be the last time you have to make a statement about this, okay?'

Though if it went to court, not the last time she'd be asked about it, surely. And, at sixteen, she'd be expected to attend, too. But no need to worry about that now. One step at a time. And Keeley seemed calm enough about everything, at least.

'That's no problem,' I said. Then I turned to Keeley myself. 'We can go down in the morning, can't we? Get it over with. Then we'll see about going to college after that, shall we?'

Keeley nodded. She looked washed out. This would start to take its toll now. It was already gone nine. Soon she'd be shattered.

She was just saying so when the male officer's radio began crackling. Then there was a voice, but it was soon drowned out by static. He stood up. 'Sorry,' he said, 'I'll just nip outside so I can take this.'

'It never stops,' Laura said. 'Non-stop, specially at this time of year.' She stood up, too. 'Still, I see there's plenty of Christmas spirit here at least. Who's the fan?' She turned to grin at me. 'It all looks very pretty. And no harm in getting ahead of the game, is there?'

Keeley rolled her eyes, and I was pleased to see the mood had lifted slightly. I even considered launching into my fairy-light tour, but Dean reappeared then and with him the business at hand.

He looked at us both in turn. 'I just thought I ought to let you both know that my boss has just informed me that Mr Burke is to be detained overnight, until his solicitor can be present. And you'll be pleased to know that Jade's been removed to a place of safety. Just temporarily, we hope, but she's safe, that's the main thing, isn't it?'

Keeley's eyes immediately filled with tears. 'Oh God, she'll be so scared,' she said. 'Can I see her? You know, just for a bit? Just to let her know I'm there? She'll be so upset. And I know *just* how that feels. *Please?*'

The officers exchanged a glance, which Keeley and I both saw. '*Please?* Or can I call her? Just to check she's okay?'

'I'm sorry, love,' Dean said. 'But at least you know she's safe. And she was happy to go – my boss said. And she knows it's just for the time being. Seems a sensible girl, if you ask me.'

I put an arm around Keeley. 'Jade will be *fine*, love. She'll have come somewhere just like this, and they'll be taking good care of her. And I tell you what I'll do,' I added, even though I knew I couldn't promise. 'I'll get straight on the phone to Danny once Dean and Laura have gone and try to find out if and when you can see her.'

'You think I might be able to?' she said, once the officers had left.

'Truthfully?' I answered. 'I really don't know. And probably won't till we know a bit more about what's going to happen. But I tell you what. Why don't you go upstairs and get into your pyjamas, and while you're doing that I will see what I can do. At the very least we should be able to get a message to her to let her know you're keen to, and that you're thinking of her. Which she'll be glad to know, won't she?'

'And make sure they give her my love?'

'As if I wouldn't. Go on. Get your 'jamas on while I get on the phone to Danny.'

Though before that I had another call to make. To Mike, to let him know it was safe to come home. Which was when it struck me that the snowball was gathering momentum. For all the talk by officer Dean about Jade being 'taken temporarily', the truth was that I knew nothing of the situation with the Burkes. It could well be that she too now no longer *had* a home.

Chapter 24

We made our statements the following morning – both of them recorded and taken down in separate rooms – but when we finally emerged there was no question of Keeley going to college; the visit to the police station seemed to have really brought home to her the enormity of the chain of events she'd set in motion. It was one thing being picked up by a patrol car, driven home and ticked off – quite another to have to contemplate the reality of what she'd started – that there would be a court case prepared and, eventually, a trial, at which she might well have to give evidence. And having been at one – Tyler's, when he was charged with attacking his stepmother – I sympathised with her. I'd feel pretty strung out as well.

Keeley didn't go in the next day or the following Monday either. She just withdrew into her shell, watching endless catch-up TV, with only me and the twinkling Christmas tree for company. And, once he got home from school each day, a newly minted Tyler, who now fully inhabited the role he should have taken in the first place

– of benign, full-of-banter big brother. I didn't ask, and I
wouldn't, not while Keeley was still with us, but I suspected
– and happily – there might be a girl involved in this pleas-
ing transformation.

But that could wait. In the meantime, the days were
growing ever shorter, and the only glimmer of brightness
on my fostering horizon was when Keeley shuffled into
the kitchen one afternoon a few days later and told me she
needed to make an apology – that she was very glad I'd put
the Christmas tree up now.

She also wrote to Jade twice. Two very long letters.
Whether Jade would be allowed to receive and read them
was quite another thing, but I didn't tell Keeley that. I
didn't tell her anything, in fact, of the little I did know,
because I'd been told I mustn't – as a potential witness she
must be starved of information in order that her testimony
couldn't be challenged in court.

One thing I did know was that, from the outset, Steve
Burke had denied all the charges. 'Entirely as we expected,'
the family liaison officer told me, when he called on the
Tuesday. 'He's a rabbit in the headlights, so it's pretty
standard at this point,' he went on, 'so don't read anything
into it. But it does mean you're perfectly entitled to hire
your own solicitor if you want to. That said, though,' he
finished, 'Jade Burke is co-operating fully with the investigation, so I doubt you'd actually need one, truth be
known.'

I wasn't sure what to make of all that, but at least his
tone was reassuring. And I was happier still when the news
came the next morning that John and Danny were going

to come round with a fuller update. 'That's good,' I said. 'We're in need of some positive news. We're all feeling very much in limbo.'

'Well, you're bound to be,' John consoled me, 'but this could all go on for months, as you know. I'd say best to keep busy and distracted.'

I've known John a long time and picked up on it straight away. He'd put the emphasis on the word 'distracted' and a new hope bubbled up. Had something changed? Did he have some news about Keeley being able to see Jade? Oh God, I hoped so. It would really give her a boost, I knew.

'I'm all distracted-out,' I said. 'And I have no more fairy lights left to deploy. Do you have a suggestion about *where* we should find that distraction? Come on, I know you're keeping something from me. Will you please spit it out?'

John laughed. 'Tomorrow. And that's all I can say. I'm still waiting for another phone call before I can be absolutely sure. I'll get back to you as soon as I can.'

It hit me like a thunderbolt. Could it be? So soon?

'You mean –'

'Tomorrow,' he said firmly. 'Now put your jaw back in place. Poker face, remember. Not a word to Keeley.'

'Phone me, yes?' I made him promise.

He promised.

'Do you think they're coming to tell us that the pervert has confessed?' Keeley mused as I stood looking out of the window the following morning, ants very much in my pants. It had snowed overnight and was still coming down now. Big lazy flakes that I'd doubted would lie, but were looking increasingly like they were intent on proving me wrong.

Under normal circumstances I would have been over the moon to see my front garden all deep and crisp and even like this, even if Christmas was still some way away. Precisely because Christmas was some way away, more accurately, invoking visions of the whole of Britain becoming one big snowdrift and of the scenes on the Christmas cards I'd already begun writing being a real actual thing rather than just whimsy.

Today, however, the snow just added to the chill of impending doom I was feeling. It had been unlike John to leave me hanging when he had something important to impart, and I was beginning to think that whatever the phone call was he'd been waiting for might have come back as bad news. They were due any minute, after all, and still he hadn't called.

'Casey?' Keeley prompted, nudging me out of my reverie. 'What d'you think? Do you think it could be that? God, I so hope so. I can't believe he really thinks he can get away with it.'

I turned towards her and gave her a tight smile. 'Who knows? But he'll have to admit it eventually, I just know it. With Jade's evidence as well as yours, it won't really matter so much if he does keep denying it anyway. In fact, once they do find some decent evidence, he'll have only made it worse for himself. The police and the courts aren't stupid. They'll see through him. And don't forget, they'll be amassing evidence as we speak, won't they? Going through his phone records and bank records and credit card statements and so on. There'll be some trail which will corroborate what you told them. There always is.'

I didn't know that for sure, of course, and if he had been very clever, and the evidence was scant, both girls might be required to give their evidence again. I knew it would be awful if it came to that.

'Anyway,' I said, spying a car finally approaching. 'We're about to find out, kiddo. John and Danny are here.'

It was John's car that pulled up, Danny unbending himself from the passenger seat and bobbing up from the far side of the car, and both yanking their collars up as they started down our path, disturbing the lovely snow with their soggy, grey footprints. 'Pop the kettle on, Keeley,' I called as I hurried to the door. 'And pop those mince pies in the oven. They look like they need them.'

Danny grinned as he stamped snow off his shoes. 'Go north, young man, they said. It'll be lovely, they said. D'you know, I think I've seen more snow in the past year than I've seen in my entire life down south. I mean, it's not even Christmas yet, for goodness sake!'

'Smells like it, though,' John said, sniffing the air as he came in. 'Casey here is the queen of the mini mince pie. From November onwards, as you'll already have noticed.'

I studied the pair of them so closely that John even noticed. 'Told you,' John said. 'I said she would burn us with her eyes, didn't I?'

I felt the heaviness in my stomach grow lighter. Then mild annoyance. Had he been keeping his good news from me on purpose?

Apparently so. We were all seated round the table before he finally confirmed it. 'Sorry, Casey,' he told me. 'I would have called, but I couldn't steal Danny's thunder.'

'What thunder?' Keeley asked. 'What exactly is going on here?'

'Lots, Keels,' Danny told her. 'We have some news for you.'

'About Jade?' Her eyes were bright now. 'Am I going to be allowed to see her?'

'Not yet,' Danny told her. 'But there's good news on that front as well. Stephen Burke has decided to change his plea.'

'Which means what?' she asked.

'That there'll be a great deal less paperwork. Which means a great deal less manpower, and a great deal less time. And, as a consequence, also a great deal less time till you can see her. So that's good, isn't it?'

'Oh, that's *is* good,' I enthused. I was warming to this now.

'You said "front",' Keeley came back immediately, sharp as ever. 'I mean it's brilliant, but you said "on that front". So what's the other front?'

Danny sat forward in his seat and cleared his throat, as if preparing to deliver a long speech. 'First of all, Keels, an apology. I know you've been through hell this last year or so, and nobody picked up on it. Not me, nor anybody else, so for that I want to say I'm truly sorry –'

'You don't have to apologise,' she said. 'I didn't tell anyone, did I? In fact, I told a bunch of lies instead. Seriously, we're cool.'

'Even so,' he went on, 'I should have picked up on *something*. And you're still going through it now, having to give statement after statement after flipping statement, and I know you're probably sick to the back teeth of it. And later on, later on today, perhaps, even, I think you and I need to sit down, or stand up, or go for a walk in the snow even, and have a bit of a chat about how we move forwards from here. And if you're not ready yet, that's fine, we can do it another day, another week, whatever. But just know, I'm here for you now, okay?'

Keeley looked stunned. 'It's fine, honest. I'm cool, Danny. It's *fine*.'

'Actually, it's not fine,' Danny said. 'You've been failed at every juncture.' And he said it with such passion that Keeley even looked at me with a 'whatttt?' kind of expression.

But I thought I got it. It was important that we all recalibrate our minds and memories. Memories of what we'd assumed, what we'd learned, what we'd thought we all knew. Plus I had an inkling he was enjoying himself, too.

Keeley grinned at him. 'Whatever you say,' she said. 'Cool. We can go for a walk after this if you really want to. But what's all this got to do with this "front" thing?'

And I was glad she'd asked, because faced with two men with twinkles in their eyes to match the tree I was fast running out of patience.

'Oh that'll be nice,' I said. 'Perfect afternoon for it, too. But, yes, go on, Danny, let's get to the juicy bits.'

I tried to ignore John's snort as I watched Danny grab a file from his backpack. 'Okay,' he said, opening it up on the dining table. 'The juicy bit it is, then.' Then he grew serious. 'Now, this might be a little difficult for you to understand, Keeley, but bear with me, okay?' He cleared his throat. 'And forgive me if this sounds blunt, but I think you're old enough for me to speak plainly. It's about when you were first taken into care and denied contact with your brothers and sisters.'

I then sat back and listened while Danny ran through our initial discussion about the mysterious Mrs Higgins, and the subsequent potentially seismic events of previous weeks – only weeks, I thought – because, after everything that had happened since, that discussion now seemed a long time ago.

And he wasn't that blunt, thankfully. Only as blunt as he needed to be, skirting around the concern, then, that she might do her siblings further harm, and plumping instead for the idea that, because she'd been so traumatised, upset and damaged by what had happened to her, they were worried about *all* of them, her included, and felt separating them would be best for their emotional health.

She didn't buy it. I wouldn't have either. 'You mean they really thought *I* –' she began. 'That I would ever *do* something like that?'

Danny held a hand up. 'Not of your own volition, Keeley. It wasn't that. It was just that –'

'I knew all along,' she said, raising her own hand. 'I *know*. I know because that sicko perve *told* me. I told you,' she said to me. 'Remember? About how he told me he knew what had happened for me to end up in care. That I was lucky they agreed to foster me, because I was already so *contaminated*. Yeah,' she said, seeing our faces. 'That was the exact word he used.'

Something crossed her features and I thought she might burst into tears then, but she didn't. Nothing like it, in fact. 'That absolute fucking *bastard*,' she said instead.

Danny winced. 'Keels, please don't think it was like that, it was –'

'That's *exactly* how it was,' she corrected him. Then she nodded, as if to herself. 'Finally,' she muttered. '*Finally*.'

And it was as if, having what she'd probably suspected all along confirmed at long last, another weight had been lifted from her. Then she raised her eyes to Danny's again. 'So go on, then,' she went on. 'What's the good news on the other front? That he's finally going to prison now?'

'Oh, I think that's probably a given,' John said.

'Better than that, Keels,' Danny said. '*Far* better than that. The news on the other front is that, if you want to, we can re-establish contact with Aaron and Courtney for you.' He chuckled then. 'What am I *saying*? I mean that you can *see* them. D'oh. *That's* what I mean. That you can *see* them. Not the little ones. Not now. We have no juris-diction there, I'm afraid. Which is not to say they can't contact you, you know, in the future. But you need to put that aside, for now, at least. However, with Aaron and Courtney … Well' – he sat back and smiled a wide, happy smile – 'Keeley, they can't *wait* to see you.' He reached out to touch her hand. 'From the horse's mouth, that is, too. Would you like that?'

Her eyes were like saucers now. 'Seriously? *Seriously*?'

'One hundred and ten per cent seriously,' Danny said.

Keeley looked at me now, her eyes brimming with as yet unshed tears. 'I don't know what to say,' she whispered. 'Seriously, is this for real?'

'Of course it's for real,' I said, almost in tears myself now. 'And you've clearly been watching way too much American TV.'

'They really said that? They even remember who I *am* now?'

'Why ever wouldn't they?' I said.

'But they were only, like, six and four. God, they'll be in *high* school. Aaron will, anyway. *Shit*. Sorry. God. What must they *look* like?'

'I can help you with that,' Danny said, rummaging in his bag again. He passed her a brown envelope. 'Pictures,' he said. 'And letters too. From both of them. And Christmas cards too, I think. Go on, open it if you want to. Or not,' he quickly added. 'Entirely up to you, Keels. You might prefer to take them off to your bedroom and look at them in private.'

But Keeley didn't prefer. 'No way. I want to look at them *now*. I've been hoping and hoping,' she said, pulling open the flap. 'That they'd turn up on Facebook. I've been searching and searching … Oh. My. God. Casey, *look*.'

So I looked, well, after a fashion, because my own eyes were full of tears now. And there they were, beaming out at us in a series of snaps and goofy selfies, the boy just like Keeley, the girl very different. But whatever the cocktail of genes the three shared, none of that mattered. Never had. Not at all.

'God, I can't see for looking,' Keeley said, brushing tears from the photos.

Which felt apt – well, for us. For all of us, as a social service. But now we did see. The whole picture. Well, almost all.

Keeley must have read my thoughts. And perhaps her own mind, as she clutched those precious photos, was inexorably drawn there. 'What about Jade? What's going to happen to her now?'

Perhaps feeling a bit sidelined, and wanting his own moment in the limelight, I swear John almost went to put his hand up before he spoke.

'Well,' he said, 'I can report I have good news on that front as well. If you can cope with so much good news all at once, that is. Can you?'

Keeley winked at me. 'Do bears live in the woods?'

Chapter 25

Christmas Eve morning, and Keeley was finally 'offskies'. Which meant I already knew it was going to be a bitter-sweet kind of day. It would be our last breakfast too – well, as Keeley's foster family, anyway – and, by popular demand, a feast of appropriately salty bacon and syrupy pancakes.

Listening to the banter between her and Tyler, by now such a feature of our everyday lives, it hardly seemed possible that it had been less than four months since this girl had fetched up and turned our lives upside down and that, now, it was odds on that we wouldn't see her again. Not any time soon, I reckoned, anyway.

Which was fair enough, and exactly as it should be.

Because she was travelling some distance. Not so far that we wouldn't be able to keep in touch in the old-fashioned way now and then – face to face rather than face to screen – and not so far that she wouldn't be able to travel into college next term either, albeit from the other direction. But certainly a far enough distance that she could put enough of the stuff between her and the foster father who'd so wickedly betrayed her.

So much had happened in the last week, it had been like the proverbial whirlwind; a state of play that the weather had been only too pleased to emulate, the snowy idyll having been replaced by milder temperatures and the sort of blowy, squally skies that sucked all the brightness out of what little daylight we were getting. The forecast was for another freeze, though, for which I couldn't wait. I'd finished all my Christmas shopping (we'd opted to get Keeley some top-of-the-range hair straighteners to replace the ones she, funnily enough, never saw again) and was happy to bed in for the duration.

But first, with Danny arriving soon to take her to her new home, we had to give her a proper send-off. The pancakes all flipped (and, to celebrate, a quartet of weak Buck's Fizzes poured) we trooped into the living room to eat our breakfast, the better to enjoy the festive glow from the still twinkling tree, now in its sixth week of occupation. Tyler scooped up the framed photograph Keeley had left on the coffee table on his way.

'God help them,' he said, passing it to her as we all sat down. 'You think they have any idea what they've let themselves in for, agreeing to have their big sister back in their lives again? I mean, like, *seriously*?' he added, mimicking her intonation with impressive accuracy.

'Shut your face, *looooser*,' Keeley answered brightly. 'Nah, I'm keeping it out so I can show it to Jade. She doesn't know what they look like yet, does she?'

Ah, the cruel twist of social media-related fate. Keeley's

smartphone ('Pretty much *all* phones are smartphones now, Mum, so you really don't need to say that' – quote by Tyler) was a thing of the past. I didn't doubt some deal would be struck at some point to enable her to get her hands on a new one – possibly via her new carer, in cahoots with Danny – but for the time being it was no longer hers and no longer under contract. Instead it was in the hands of whoever minded the local police property storeroom, where, having been divested of all its crucial information, it was stuffed in an evidence bag, part of the ongoing investigation.

In the meantime, apart from the odd online session with Tyler – with necessary *sub judice* related legal constraints – Keeley was a bit starved of her virtual world. And if it hadn't been exactly rosy it had definitely added value. She'd been working all the harder on her college courses as a consequence. 'Might even get good enough to be allowed access to the barnet,' as Tyler had it re her cutting his precious hair.

For now, though, it wasn't just Keeley who was off to pastures new and distant. It was Zoe Sanders (formally Burke) and Jade too. To say I'd been knocked for six by this revelation was understatement indeed. Indeed, when Danny first shared the news that Zoe wanted to have Keeley back with her I thought he was winding me up. Either that or that he'd been at the cooking sherry.

But he hadn't been joking. That was exactly what Keeley's former foster mum most wanted. There was, of necessity, a frank debrief, with no beating about the bush. She carried enormous guilt and was keen to make amends.

She knew that, longer term, Keeley was determined to be given her independence, but wouldn't all their immediate futures be better if she and Jade were reunited under the same roof? And it wasn't just about sisterly bonding either. A case such as this was going to attract a huge amount of media attention, particularly when Stephen Burke's trial got under way. And couldn't they all better support each other if they were actually *with* each other? And needless to say, Danny was quick to agree.

I was even more taken aback that Keeley agreed with the plan so readily. After all, the way Keeley had described Zoe Burke, I'd had her down (with the usual allowance I generally make for teenage ranting and hyperbole) as a cross between a shop-window mannequin and drying paint, not to mention a purveyor of unsolicited and terrible gravy.

Not so, it seemed. Keeley, remarkably pragmatic now, and happy to keep an open mind, was, she said, open to the idea that she might have misjudged her, not to mention able to accept that their lack of empathy might have more than a little to do with the way Stephen Burke had manipulated the situation, painting Keeley as a sexually precocious predatory young female who'd set her cap at him – while he of course, ever the caring professional, kept her, with great diplomacy, at a prudent arm's length.

It was horrible to even contemplate how the ripples of his addiction spread their poison, even worse to know how he must have seen the advantages of taking a girl like Keeley into his home. And, in reality, Zoe Burke was yet another of his victims. Though Mike and I had both had several 'how could she not have known *something*?' moments in the early days following Keeley's disclosures, it turned out that we were wrong. No one would ever know for sure, of course, but the police told us they were a hundred per cent positive Zoe Burke really hadn't had a clue that her husband was a sexual deviant, not least because the 'heroic' adoptive and foster father been such a devious master of manipulation. The proverbial big bad wolf in sheep's clothing.

Zoe Burke had therefore been devastated when the evidence was laid bare before her, and the ongoing investigation revealed, time and time again, just how cleverly he'd covered his tracks down the years. And when the peepholes he'd created were apparently shown to her, Zoe Burke stopped being a Burke – media attention was already by now happening – and began divorce proceedings that same day.

Not that it had been a simple process. In the weeks leading up to Christmas there had been many meetings and interviews, before it was established that Zoe Burke could continue as a foster carer, and for her to gain interim custody of her adopted daughter Jade. Only then was she returned to her.

It was at that point that, presumably after discussing it at length with Jade, she'd suggested Keeley return to her also. Mediation then followed, so they could talk through their respective issues, and following this came the news that Keeley was happy for that to happen – at least till she'd gained her Level 1 Hair and Beauty qualification. 'Then I'm definitely offskies,' she'd told me. And, yes, she might well be. But hopefully 'offskies' into a job and a brighter future.

For now, though, she had an exciting couple of days ahead. A move to a new home, being reunited with her foster sister, then, on Boxing Day, a visit to another foster family – the home where her younger siblings lived. Up to now she'd seen them once under supervision, for an emotional hour at a contact centre across town, but their next meeting was to be at their home.

'It's like I'm having two Christmases,' she'd trilled happily. 'I can't wait!' Though being Keeley, she couldn't resist a Keeley-style rejoinder. 'Even though it's been Christmas here, like, for flipping *ever*.'

Fair enough. And entirely as it should be.

Epilogue

Stephen Burke had no choice but to change his plea to guilty. And had done so even before being presented with any incontrovertible evidence. No, the damning testimonies from both girls had turned out to be sufficient for him to realise that – to paraphrase Tyler – the game was up.

We didn't spend any time following the case or trial. Mike and I, to put it mildly, were keen to move on, not least because we didn't want it to be tea-table discussion with Tyler, and, more generally, having such horrors swirling round your brain is not generally conducive to a happy mind. Or, indeed, an aid to restful sleep. Though we were, of course, told about the outcome. Stephen Burke was convicted of several sexual-abuse-related charges and went on to be sentenced to a lengthy spell in jail.

Of more interest to us was Keeley's ongoing well-being. Despite waving her off with high hopes for that much-deserved brighter future, I did spend the first couple of weeks in January feeling anxious that the 'offskies' might come to pass sooner rather than later, as she adapted to being back in Zoe Burke's care.

But the silence remained golden, and when I next heard from Danny, in late January, he was quick to reassure me that everything was going as intended – Keeley reported that she was happy, she was regularly attending college, that she had a new, if less grand, smartphone and – Danny was apparently to make sure I knew this – 'awesomely straight and glossy hair'.

'Anyway, I'm in the area,' he went on to say, 'and I thought I'd stop by to update you properly, if you're free?'

Which tickled me – I had really come to respect Danny professionally – and the fact that he took the trouble to do that. He would go far.

'Of course,' I replied. It was January. It was grey. It was possibly that day billed as being the most miserable of the year, even. Probably was. It was certainly cold. The kind of iron, bitter cold that January does best. We duly fixed up a time a couple of hours hence. 'I'll have the coffee on,' I told him.

He laughed. 'And the posh biscuits? You set the bar, so I'm banking on you …'

So it was that, a couple of hours later, I was sitting in the kitchen with Riley, who was just gathering up her things to leave, when a car slid smoothly to a stop outside the house.

Though it wasn't me who'd seen this. It was Riley who reported it.

'Oh, that'll just be Danny,' I told her.

She'd smiled then. 'You sure, Mum? Looks more like a bunch of out-of-season trick or treaters to me.'

'What?' I said, standing up and joining her at the window. There to see, coming down my front path, a trio of unfamiliar children, all togged up in what looked like home-knitted scarves and bobble hats and mittens. Somewhat bemused, I scanned their faces, wondering who they might be. And was still doing so when I opened the front door.

At which point Keeley popped out from wherever she'd been hiding.

'Surpriiiiiise!' she squealed, throwing her arms around me, in a chilly bear-hug.

She let me go then, and introduced the other three red-cheeked visitors. 'This is Jade. But you knew that. And this is Aaron and this is Courtney ... and' – she looked back to where Danny was now ambling down the path – 'this was *all* my idea. And Danny said we should trick you, and, well, here we are!'

Which is why I always keep a stock of posh biscuits.

TOPICS FOR READING-GROUP DISCUSSION

1. Grooming a child for the specific intention of gaining their trust in order to commit a sexual act with them is against the law. However, despite calls for the government to make this law enforceable, a grey area remains. An offence is only committed if the adult defendant knew without doubt that the victim was under the age of sixteen. How can this be proven?

2. What steps do you feel could be put in place to ensure that adults cannot communicate online with children in order to groom them?

3. In this story, Keeley, the fostered child, was herself using a false persona online to entice men into buying her gifts. Although this is not exactly grooming in the legal sense, what she was doing was very close to what we consider grooming to be. Do you think young people see such things as part and parcel of life in the internet age?

4. With computers and smartphones now an integral part of life, what role do you think schools should play in keeping children safe online? Are they doing enough?

5. Recently there have been a lot of vigilante-type groups set up online showing video clips of members of anti-grooming campaigns posing as young girls to entrap groomers, then 'catching' the perpetrators and making citizens' arrests. Do you agree with the tactics of such groups, or do you think that the police should be doing this themselves?

6. One way to stop people setting up fake identities online is to make it extremely difficult to create them on social media, perhaps by requiring traceable ID such as a National Insurance number. Do you think this is desirable? And if so, would it be possible to enforce it?

CASEY WATSON

One woman determined to
make a difference.

Read Casey's poignant
memoirs and be inspired.

Adrianna arrives on Casey's doorstep with no possessions, no English and no explanation

It will be a few weeks before Casey starts getting the shocking answers to her questions . . .

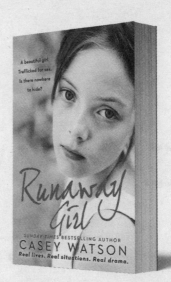

RUNAWAY GIRL

Bella's father is on a ventilator, fighting for his life, while her mother is currently on remand in prison, charged with his attempted murder.

Bella is the only witness.

THE SILENT WITNESS

Flip is being raised by her alcoholic mother, and comes to Casey after a fire at their home

Flip has Foetal Alcohol Syndrome (FAS), but it soon turns out that this is just the tip of the iceberg ...

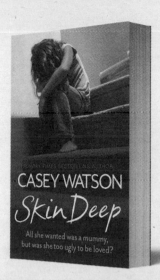

SKIN DEEP

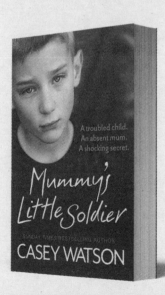

Leo isn't a bad lad, but his frequent absences from school mean he's on the brink of permanent exclusion

Leo is clearly hiding something, and Casey knows that if he is to have any kind of future, it's up to her to find out the truth.

MUMMY'S LITTLE SOLDIER

What is the secret behind Imogen's silence?

Discover the shocking and devastating past of a child with severe behavioural problems.

THE GIRL WITHOUT A VOICE

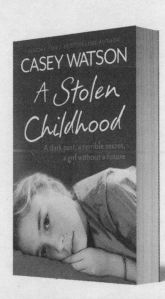

Kiara appears tired and distressed, and the school wants Casey to take her under her wing for a while

On the surface, everything points to a child who is upset that her parents have separated. The horrific truth, however, shocks Casey to the core.

A STOLEN CHILDHOOD

A teenage mother and baby in need of a loving home

At fourteen, Emma is just a child herself – and one who's never been properly mothered.

A LAST KISS FOR MUMMY

Eleven-year-old Tyler has stabbed his stepmother and has nowhere to go

With his birth mother dead and a father who doesn't want him, what can be done to stop his young life spiralling out of control?

NOWHERE TO GO

A young girl secretly caring for her mother

Abigail has been dealing with pressures no child should face. Casey has the difficult challenge of helping her to learn to let go.

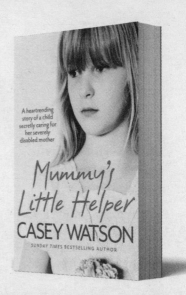

MUMMY'S LITTLE HELPER

Two boys with an unlikely bond

With Georgie and Jenson, Casey is facing her toughest test yet.

BREAKING THE SILENCE

Abused siblings who do not know what it means to be loved

With new-found security and trust, Casey helps Ashton and Olivia to rebuild their lives.

LITTLE PRISONERS

Branded 'vicious and evil', eight-year-old Spencer asks to be taken into care

Casey and her family are disgusted: kids aren't born evil. Despite the challenges Spencer brings, they are determined to help him find a loving home.

TOO HURT TO STAY

Five-year-old Justin was desperate and helpless

Six years after being taken into care, Justin has had 20 failed placements. Casey and her family are his last hope.

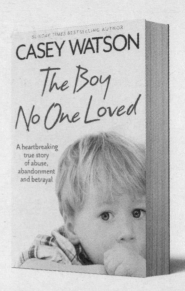

A damaged girl haunted by her past

Sophia pushes Casey to the limits, threatening the safety of the whole family. Can Casey make a difference in time?

AVAILABLE AS E-BOOK ONLY

Cameron is a sweet boy who seems happy in his skin – making him rather different from most of the other children Casey has cared for

But what happens when Cameron disappears? Will Casey's worst fears be realised?

CASEY WATSON
SUNDAY TIMES BESTSELLING AUTHOR

Just a Boy

An inspiring and heartwarming
short story

JUST A BOY

SUNDAY TIMES BESTSELLING AUTHOR

CASEY WATSON

Scarlett's Secret

A real-life
short story
by Casey
Watson

Jade and Scarlett, seventeen-year-old twins, share a terrible secret

Can Casey help them come to terms with the truth and rediscover their sibling connection?

SCARLETT'S SECRET

AVAILABLE AS E-BOOK ONLY

Nathan has a sometime alter ego called Jenny who is the only one who knows the secrets of his disturbed past

But where is Jenny when she is most needed?

NO PLACE FOR NATHAN

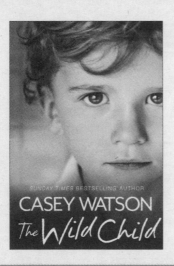

Angry and hurting, eight-year-old Connor is from a broken home

As streetwise as they come, he's determined to cause trouble. But Casey is convinced there is a frightened child beneath the swagger.

THE WILD CHILD

Six-year-old Darby is naturally distressed at being removed from her parents just before Christmas

And when the shocking and sickening reason is revealed, a Happy New Year seems an impossible dream as well ...

THE LITTLE PRINCESS

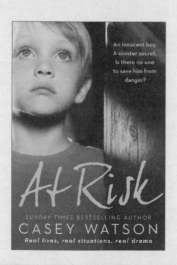

Adam is brought to Casey while his mum recovers in hospital – just for a few days

But a chance discovery reveals that Casey has stumbled upon something altogether more sinister ...

AT RISK

FEEL HEART.
FEEL HOPE.
READ CASEY.

Discover more about Casey Watson.
Visit www.caseywatson.co.uk

Find Casey Watson on &